Stephen Platten is Bishop of Wakefiel
Theological College. Later, he was the A
ary for Ecumenical Affairs before becc
Stephen is the author of *Pilgrims* and *Au...... . ... , ...
and editor of several other books, including *Rebuilding Jerusalem: The Church's hold on hearts and minds* and, with Christopher Lewis, *Dreaming Spires? Cathedrals in a new age*, both published by SPCK. In 2005, he was appointed Chairman of the Liturgical Commission.

C000067961

VOCATION

Singing the Lord's song

Stephen Platten

First published in Great Britain in 2007

Society for Promoting Christian Knowledge
36 Causton Street
London SW1P 4ST

Copyright © Stephen Platten 2007

British Library Cataloguing-in-Publication Data
A catalogue record for this book is available from the British Library

ISBN 978–0–281–05962–1

1 3 5 7 9 10 8 6 4 2

Typeset by Graphicraft Ltd, Hong Kong
Printed in Great Britain by Ashford Colour Press

Produced on paper from sustainable forests

*For Brother Edward SSF and the Society of St Francis
who more than anyone else lived out for me
the vocation of God's Church in Jesus Christ*

Contents

Preface   ix

Introduction   xi

1   Both sides, now
    The world   1

2   American pie
    The world in crisis   14

3   Imagine
    God   28

4   The way old friends do
    The Church   41

5   Bridge over troubled water
    Priesthood   56

6   Angels
    Deacons as messengers   71

7   You raise me up
    Other vocations: the religious life, readers   84

    Coda
    Offering, worship, Eucharist,
    contemplation, silence   97

Notes   102

Index   107

*How shall we sing the L*ORD*'s song in a strange land?*
(Psalm 137.4, AV)

Preface

Books – even short books like this – do not just happen. They begin with the germ of an idea which is then watered and nourished largely by others. The germ of the idea I owe, as indeed so much else, to Rosslie, my wife. I was approaching my first ever study leave rather like a train bursting out of a tunnel with little idea where the points were going to take me and with apparently no control over the signal box. Rosslie suggested that, among other things, I might write a short, popular book. Having for once time to reflect I decided that the book might be about the vocation of God's Church and might be addressed to those, among others, who feel they may be being prodded in the direction of some sort of public ministry.

Both my sons, who are ordained, offered helpful comments on my original plan and did so in the twinkling of an eye. Joanna Moriarty and Gordon Lamont from SPCK helped me sharpen the plan still further. Both Stephen Spencer and Aidan Platten read through the entire text and made encouraging and constructively critical suggestions as I wrote. Both Jane Butterfield and Marlene Beresford have typed endlessly, editing the text and producing the original copy – beautifully laid out as ever. Simon Beresford, Gregory Platten and Gillian Straine also kindly read the text. The senior staff of Wakefield Diocese, and especially Tony Robinson, made it all possible by looking after things while I was on sabbatical. Errors and infelicities undoubtedly remain, but they form part of my own contribution. I am enormously grateful to all whom I have mentioned and who have helped this book come to birth in relatively double-quick time.

Stephen Platten

Introduction

As a youngster I remember yearning to go on the exciting holidays that some of my school friends were taking. We spent our holidays fairly traditionally – in England, on a beach, and with a bucket and spade. Others seemed to go to exotic places. Looking back we can all now see that a revolution was then in the making. Cheap package holidays to the Mediterranean were just the beginning of the tourism explosion. Now perhaps more people holiday abroad than in their home country. This has itself led to a radical change in many people's perception of the world. We see our own country differently once we have travelled in other lands. We can see too how those lands themselves have changed throughout their history. One example will suffice. Travel to North Africa and you see Leptis Magna and the ruins of Carthage. Here are the remnants of one of the earliest Christian civilizations. It gave birth to many of the early saints, and was the homeland of the great St Augustine of Hippo, one of the makers of the Western Christian tradition. But to be a Christian there now is to live in a sort of exile. Similarly Muslims visiting southern Spain would feel parallel emotions. The great mosque in Cordoba has a baroque cathedral inserted into its heart. Muslims will feel themselves in exile in a strange land. That is the emotion evoked by that psalm verse quoted as the epigraph to this book.

Now, of all the psalms in the psalter, Psalm 137 may seem a very odd choice from which to begin a book on the Church in the contemporary world. Remaining with the Authorized Version, the final verse, verse 9, runs: 'Happy shall he be, that taketh and dasheth thy little ones against the stones.' It has become virtually a classical text when discussing how the Bible can, or indeed cannot, be used in the present day. What can theologians make of the Bible's authority? What might this say, either to society as a whole or more specifically to the Church, about the Bible's contribution to moral thought? That in itself is a significant issue, but it is not the issue upon which this book intends to reflect. Nevertheless the fourth verse of that same psalm, printed out above, may speak more directly to the purpose of this book. For the main theme with which we shall engage is the vocation of the wider Christian community, that is of the Church, and of individual ministers within that Church. So, that resonant fourth verse picks up a mood which is often there today within the various Christian communities of Western Europe. As with the situation of the psalmist, so with us too there is a feeling of living in exile. It is not, of course, a geographical exile, but instead something of a cultural exile. Often it does feel that witnessing to, living or indeed speaking about the Christian faith is foreign to many within European culture. It does feel as if we are 'singing the Lord's song in a strange land'.

If this is true, then it presents more than sufficient difficulties to the Church as a whole in its task as acting as a beacon to the gospel within the wider world. It has become perhaps more difficult still to reflect upon the Church's vocation and the vocation of those who are ordained within the Church. Frequently we find ourselves being so busy trying to offer a 'reason for the faith that is within us' – that is, an apologetic for the Christian gospel – that we are diverted from a more particular focus upon the question of vocation itself.

The seeds of the enterprise which has stimulated the writing of this short book, then, issue from a feeling that there is need for something which might speak directly to this sense of vocation, and which might also be helpful to those considering whether they should offer themselves as candidates for the ordained priesthood, the diaconate, the religious life, reader ministry, or some other formal ministry or offering of themselves within God's Church. So this aims to be a book which begins with a vision of the Christian life and of Christian ministry rather than simply a technical discussion of the theological roots of ministry and vocation. It certainly does reflect upon aspects of the theology of ministry, but it begins with people's experience and most notably their experiences of the world. The last book to do this in a really visionary way was Archbishop Michael Ramsey's *The Christian Priest Today* (SPCK, 1985). That book remains a classic and is effectively irreplaceable. While it issues from a series of expanded and revised ordination charges given by the Archbishop, it soon develops into an integrated vision of the priestly life. It concentrates entirely on priesthood and not on other forms of representative ministry. Some of the key elements of the context of that vision of the Christian life have changed in the past 40 years and so the assumption behind this present book is that there is now more to be said.

So, the following pages will first and foremost reflect upon the vocation of all God's people, that is, all who would follow the way of God as seen in Jesus Christ. That vocation begins with the gospel itself and notably the pattern of life lived out by Jesus. We find that pattern described variously in the four Gospels; we see the pattern described in a different way in the Pauline writings, in the other letters in the New Testament, and in the Acts of the Apostles and the Apocalypse of John.

The pattern lived out by Jesus and within the apostolic communities is one which is repeated and developed in the early Church and more generally in the life of the great variety of Christian communities down the centuries. Moving on from that point theologically, catholic Christendom also developed a theology of both Church and ministry. This theology aimed to give shape to the manner in which Christians should live out the gospel and indeed through this to point others towards the gospel within wider society. For the Church does not live for itself. In other words, at no point should or indeed *could* the Church live out the gospel in isolation from wider culture. Some of the more austere monastic traditions attempted this to a degree. Even they, however, found themselves reacting to and being fashioned by the surrounding culture. Indeed, this impact of the ambient culture upon the monasteries was one of the stimulants to the foundation of renewed patterns of religious life both during the Middle Ages and indeed much later on, in the nineteenth and even twentieth centuries. So, the Cistercian rule was a revised and 'tougher' version of the Benedictine rule of which it is effectively itself a mutation. Benedictines, Cluniacs, Cistercians, Franciscans and Dominicans would all have seen themselves in different ways as attempting still to 'sing the Lord's song in a strange land'.

Having moved from a neutral view of the world to a view of the world created, redeemed and sustained by God, we find ourselves reflecting upon this within the Church. The Church attempts to live out the pattern of life established by God in Jesus Christ. From here – that is, from within the Church – our reflections will lead us into considering the more specific understanding of an ordained ministry, and notably of the priesthood and the diaconate. Nonetheless, the key point remains. Vocation begins with all who would live the Christian life. This requires a real understanding of what the Church is for and indeed what it is called to be. Vocation, then, is not simply a personal direct line to God, even though since the Reformation and the Counter-Reformation it has often seemed to be so. Emphasis upon the individual's personal relationship with Christ emerged in both traditions and often submerged the truth that humanity is created and redeemed in solidarity and not only through individual lives. This is a point made abundantly clear in the writings of St Paul, and notably in his letter to the Romans. In recovering that sense of solidarity both within our humanity, and through the Church of God, vocation, then, needs to be seen rather differently. It now becomes an offering of an individual or individuals within the community of the Church to see whether their particular talents, skills, character and abilities are such as to resonate with the vocation to which the whole of God's Church is called. We are called to sing the Lord's song in chorus and not alone. This means the broadest possible engagement between humanity and the God who is Creator, Redeemer and Sustainer within God's world – hence the title of this book.

The musical theme does not, however, end with the book's title. Each of the chapter headings is also taken from a 'classic' or popular song from the different decades of the past 50 years; this is deliberate – the aim is to begin in a place which is unquestionably worldly. Popular songs may seem an odd place from which to start, to seek after titles for chapters in a book on Christian vocation and priesthood. However, it is often when one is at one's most visionary and idealistic that one is touched by such romantic feelings and reflections, by music and song. Indeed sometimes, as we shall see, the stories surrounding the writing of these songs themselves touch upon significant issues for those song-writers within their own lives. Such vision and idealism often prompt thoughts within individuals, to think of offering themselves, first to God and then to others. The 1960s, from which the earliest song titles have come, were visionary times; many may have felt that it was an unfinished or, in some cases, a superficial vision which emerged, but there was a real sense of seeing the world in a new way. One song popu-larized by the Beatles began 'Roll over Beethoven and tell Tchaikovsky the news . . .' In other words, we now live in a new dispensation – we no longer have simply to put up with the stuff with which we were earlier fed, or indeed which we somehow imbibed with our mother's milk. There was even a feeling of revolution around. That sense of revolution was there too with the birth of the new covenant in Jesus Christ. It has been there whenever people have been challenged by the gospel of which Jesus was the incarnation and which he first lived.

The use of imagery rooted in song has a further resonance. Down the centuries the Church has encapsulated and even passed on the faith in song. Psalmody, hymns, anthems, choruses and 'worship songs' all attempt to do this. The Magnificat, or Song of Mary, in the New Testament does something similar, as does the ancient hymn of praise known as the Te Deum. Even the creeds are often *sung* within worship rather than simply said. In every one of these cases the Church is 'singing the Lord's song'. How then can our contemporary world stimulate us to sing that song again, with an added freshness in our generation?

In the context of our present culture, using some of the material from that culture as a 'jumping off' point, we shall seek to answer this ques-tion. We shall attempt to describe something of the continuing vocation of the Church in the world. Who are we called to be, and what is the impact of the gospel we are called to live? We shall begin with that world as it is, as our point of departure, and return to it at the end of our reflections. On the way we shall discover how that world is enriched when seen undeniably as part of God's creation and as the focus of his redeeming care.

1

Both sides, now

The world

———◦•◦———

Moons and Junes and Ferris wheels
The dizzy dancing way you feel
As ev'ry fairy tale comes real –
I've looked at love that way.

But now it's just another show –
You leave 'em laughing when you go
And if you care, don't let 'em know –
Don't give yourself away.

I've looked at love from both sides now
From give and take, and still somehow
It's love's illusions I recall
I really don't know love at all.[1]

Joni Mitchell's 'Both sides, now', borrowing as it does from the folk tradition, is no bad place to start in reflecting upon our world. In its three verses it looks at life, love and the world; it focuses us as an audience upon the ambiguous nature of the world and of our own experience of it. Rather evocatively, she begins, in her first verse, with clouds – as the cynic says, every silver lining has a cloud!

Bows and flows of angel hair
And ice-cream castles in the air
And feather canyons everywhere
I've looked at clouds that way.

But now it's clouds' illusions she recalls, Mitchell tells us. Then, in the verse above she moves on to love. Her subject is, of course, romantic love, but the experience of which she speaks has a much wider significance.

This wider significance is captured particularly sharply in those lines which run:

> And if you care, don't let 'em know –
> Don't give yourself away.

The world is a tough place and people get hurt. All human beings carry within themselves their own insecurities. One means of protection from the vulnerability produced by such insecurities is to construct defence mechanisms for ourselves – 'so if you care, don't let 'em know'. The result of this is that individuals easily become 'well defended', as the jargon goes. It is safest not to let others know too much about what is really going on inside us. Ultimately, of course, this leads to a good deal of pretence. We find ourselves dealing only with that element of others which they *allow to be seen* or with which they are happy for us to inter-act. Some elements of this can extend into relationships between groups, sub-cultures and even nations. Nations also easily become defensive and, indeed, through that very process, aggressive too; we are then well on the way to conflict and bloodshed. We must be cautious here, however, for relationships between individuals and groups are not universally transferable between each other. People act differently when they are in community – and not always for the better.

What precisely is it, then, that causes almost all of us at some point to act in this defensive manner? Part of it is simply that the world – and that includes our dealings and relationships within that world – is an ambiguous place. This ambiguity reaches all the way down to the nature of creation itself. In pointing to this ambiguity we might begin with a case in point. On Boxing Day 2004, early on in the day, the Western world heard just a hint of the news of a tidal wave affecting the nations around the Indian Ocean. As the day wore on, so the reports indeed confirmed a devastating tsunami which eventually claimed the lives of hundreds of thousands of people and affected the economies and infra-structures of a number of countries in a most appalling manner. No one – apart possibly from God – could have been blamed for this cata-strophe. It is part of the way the world is. The movement of the tectonic plates which make up our planet, which help to give it its beauty and which also form the foundation for the fertile land on which we are nourished, can also bring about relatively unpredictable and terrifying events – 'acts of God', as the insurance companies would have it. Earth-quakes and volcanic activity are facts of life. The explosion of Krakatoa in the late nineteenth century, which eliminated an entire island from the landscape, happened in the same part of the world as the recent tsunami, but many other similar earthquakes and eruptions could be catalogued across the world. Similarly the existence of awful diseases – the recent spread of HIV and AIDS in Africa is a horrifying example – present similar scenarios. Humanity is learning how to combat such disease, but can hardly be blamed for the existence of disease and pandemic.

Alongside these natural disasters and diseases stand those other calamities which humanity somehow seems to bring upon itself. In recent years the various wars within the Middle East have all too frequently filled our television screens. Even the enormities of Saddam Hussein, however, pale into insignificance in contrast with some of the other human catastrophes within the twentieth century. The 1916 Armenian genocide claimed between one and two million people; this is a brutal and horrifying fact and some within Turkey still seek to obliterate any evidence that Armenians ever lived in this part of Eurasia.[2] Denial is their only defence. The documentation for the holocaust, or Shoah, during the Second World War is relatively plentiful; six million European Jews died as a result of concentration and extermination camps. Josef Stalin was probably responsible for the death of more than 14 million Kulaks, many of them dying of starvation by the roadside in southern Russia or the Ukraine.[3] Finally, a recent joint biography of Mao Zedong suggests that he was responsible for the death of more than 70 million of his countrymen; 27 million died through execution or through the conditions in prison and labour camps, and the others died of starvation because of the policies pursued by the regime.[4] It would only be depressing to catalogue more of these hideous crimes against humanity. This is sufficient to make the point about the negative elements which go to make up part of our world's ambiguity.

We have seen too that neither the nature of creation itself nor the fallenness of human nature can be used as the focus of all the blame. On some occasions there will be elements of both. So in the case of the 2004 tsunami, commentators have reflected that this was a catastrophe which was waiting to happen. Seismologists know that the strain between plates in that part of the world is such as to ensure further earthquakes, eruptions and tidal waves. They argued, therefore, that placing a network of electronic monitors under the sea and on the land could have helped predict relatively accurately when such a shift was about to occur. This would have allowed the authorities within nations to take action to move populations – often just a few miles back from the coast – to prevent loss of life on a significant scale. Such precautions have already been taken around the rim of the Pacific Ocean. Another rather different example presses home the point. One of the early catastrophes of the twentieth century which provoked reflection about this mixture of natural and human responsibility and causation was the sinking of the *Titanic*. The iceberg was ultimately to blame for the loss of life, but might not better seamanship have avoided the disaster? Or could better maritime engineering have helped? Certainly engineers have noted that the construction of the hull of the *Titanic* was likely to have made some form of catastrophe a possibility, if not a certainty. Poet and novelist Thomas Hardy, writing close to the events, was even prepared to give the disaster, with its obvious ambiguities, a metaphysical or even religious slant. So he wrote of the collision of the great ship with the iceberg:

> No mortal eye could see
> The intimate welding of their later history,
>
> Or sign that they were bent
> By paths coincident
> On being anon twin halves of one August event,
>
> Till the Spinner of the Years
> Said 'Now!' And each one hears,
> And consummation comes, and jars two hemispheres.[5]

Hardy, then, was well aware of this profound ambiguity and, as in other poems and in his novels, appears to attribute such catastrophes to some form of capricious being, the Spinner of the Years, who stands behind the universe and its operation. Hardy was no conventional atheist or unbeliever but rather struggled to hold together the supreme beauty and benevolence of much of creation (of which he was a remarkable painter in words) with the apparent cruelty of the universe, sometimes as an account of human evil and sometimes because of the natural world.

Everything, however, is not bad news, despite the apparent efforts of the media to suggest as much. Alongside a catalogue of disasters within our world one can also place a very different picture of extraordinary beauty and richness. Astronauts looking back to 'planet Earth' have spoken lyrically of the beauty of our world. Or, more within our own reach, there is the beauty of so many different landscapes – many people speak of their joy in standing on a high point and surveying the landscape. Within the UK, the wild scenery of the Scottish Highlands, the tranquillity of the English Lakes, the soft folds of the North and South

Downs and the diminutive rolling hills of the Lincolnshire Wolds all stand apart as what are now designated officially as 'areas of outstanding natural beauty'. Even the dark heathlands of Dartmoor or the tough scenery of the Scottish islands have about them a haunting beauty. Moving further afield, still more striking scenery can hardly be gainsaid for its panoramic glory: the Grand Canyon, the Angel Falls in South America, the Himalayas or the Great Barrier Reef could never have been constructed through human efforts.

Nonetheless, human artefacts too testify to a beauty that most of us would be unable to imagine in our own minds. The buildings and gardens of Louis XIV's great palace at Versailles, the ancient Forum in Rome, the Sydney Harbour bridge, the vaulting of King's College Chapel in Cambridge, Venice's canals and the pyramids of Egypt are but half a dozen dazzling examples of the possibilities of human creativity. Even something as random as the skyline of New York's Manhattan has its own unique beauty. Then, along with all this, comes the beauty of the atomic and also the organic world of nature. The variety represented within the animal kingdom and the ways in which animal and plant life operate, both as individual organisms and indeed mutually relating with each other, are another obvious source for wonder. To this may be added the remarkable developments of medical science, which have issued from human genius and inventiveness. Science, as it has developed, has brought with it its own sense of beauty. These limited catalogues, then, set out for us briefly the other side of the coin of creation. In no sense is the world all bad news – far from it – but it is undoubtedly ambiguous and this is a fact that has been there from the beginning. Perhaps one of the most oft-quoted summaries of this fact, such that it has now almost become a rather tired cliché, is that couplet from the end of Max Ehrmann's 'Desiderata':

> with all its sham, drudgery and broken dreams,
> it is still a beautiful world.[6]

But the sharpness of this ambiguity is seen far more starkly by standing alongside each other two or more pieces of outstanding literature. So first, the dark side of our world, seen through the reflections of Shakespeare's doomed Prince of Denmark. Hamlet remarks:

> How weary, stale, flat and unprofitable
> Seem to me all the uses of this world.
> Fie on't! O fie! 'tis an unweeded garden,

5

That grows to seed, things rank and gross in nature
Possess it merely.[7]

Hamlet, on the way to taking his own life, reflects on the negativity of the world in which he has been placed. But then there is Francis Kilvert, also doomed to far too short a life, looking out over the Welsh Marches from the edge of England:

> The Black Mountains were invisible, being wrapped in clouds, and I saw one very white brilliant cloud where the mountains ought to have been. This cloud grew more white and dazzling every moment, till a clearer burst of sunlight scattered the mists and revealed the truth . . . and I stood rooted to the ground, struck with amazement and overwhelmed at the extraordinary splendour of this marvellous spectacle . . . one's first involuntary thought in the presence of these magnificent sights is to lift up the heart to God and humbly thank him for having made the earth so beautiful.[8]

Here is Kilvert, then, on this particular day, seeing well beyond 'clouds' illusions' to a world so breathtakingly beautiful that he is quite taken out of himself. On this occasion it is literally the clouds which help to make it a breathtaking scene. There are many other places in his diary from whence there issues a similar feeling, but equally there are moments of pathos and sadness which do not ignore the darker side of our planet and the experience which it affords us.

As has already been hinted, this ambiguity within our world extends well into our humanity too. This is obvious in the references we have made to war and genocide, but it is equally clear in the lives of any one of us, at least in these sharp moments of honesty about our strengths and our weaknesses, or indeed about our failures and aspirations. This was most eloquently put into verse by Alexander Pope in his *Essay on Man*. So in one passage he captures the dilemma succinctly:

> Know then thyself, presume not God to scan;
> The proper study of mankind is man.
> Placed on this isthmus of a middle state,
> A being darkly wise, and rudely great;
> With too much knowledge for the sceptic side,
> With too much weakness for the stoic's pride,
> He hangs between; in doubt to act or rest,
> In doubt to deem himself a god, or beast;
> In doubt his mind or body to prefer,

> Born to die, and reas'ning but to err;
> Alike in ignorance, his reason such,
> Whether he thinks too little, or too much.

Pope captures, then, the ambiguity of our world and of our experience as it is clearly projected within our own nature. For what Pope describes is nothing less than the ambiguous nature of our humanity. Later on he encapsulates it even more sharply:

> Created half to rise, and half to fall;
> Great lord of all things, yet a prey to all;
> Sole judge of truth, in endless error hurled;
> The glory, jest, and riddle of the world.

In the New Testament, St Paul focuses this sharply and pithily in his letter to the Romans:

> We know that the law is spiritual; but I am carnal, sold under sin. I do not understand my own actions. For I do not do what I want, but I do the very thing I hate. Now if I do what I do not want, I agree that the law is good. So then it is no longer I that do it, but sin which dwells within me. For I know that nothing good dwells within me, that is, in my flesh. I can will what is right, but I cannot do it. For I do not do the good I want, but the evil that I do not want is what I do. Now if I do what I do not want, it is no longer I that do it, but sin which dwells within me. So I find it to be a law that when I want to do right, evil lies close at hand.[9]

Paul's reflection of his own experience is almost certainly one with which we could all resonate. Here, then, is the world into which we are all born and to which we needs must respond. It is a world which certainly offers hints of real hope and of the divine but not, as Hardy noted, unambiguously so. Even Wordsworth, writing at the zenith of the Romantic movement (when Coleridge, his erstwhile friend, would see the poetic medium as the very voice of the divine), saw something of the world's ambiguity:

> There was a time when meadow, grove, and stream,
> The earth, and every common sight,
>   To me did seem
>   Apparelled in celestial light,

> The glory and the freshness of a dream.
> It is not now as it hath been of yore;

Wordsworth does not lose entirely the aspiration and hope, and in contrast to Pope can describe the soul as:

> But trailing clouds of glory do we come
> From God, who is our home.[10]

Nevertheless we have seen the other darker side too and there is much within our world and our experience for which we might hope and seek redemption. What do we say then of those clouds of darkness and illusion, and how might we set out on a journey to glean from both the 'trailing clouds of glory' and the darker clouds of illusion some sense of what God is calling out of the Church in the world?

Before moving on to set out the next steps of our journey, let us pause for one moment at those dark and illusory clouds, the clouds which cause Joni Mitchell to retreat into herself in order that she might not give herself away. Are those clouds so dark and impenetrable as to extinguish all hope in the meaninglessness of a capricious, sterile or perhaps demonic world? Even from our own experience, we might hold back from such hopelessness. There are those extraordinary shafts of nobility glimpsed in the lives of those facing the direst of diseases. Michael Mayne, sometime Dean of Westminster, set out on writing a reflective memoir when in the midst of it he was overtaken by the blackness of a cancer of the jaw. Out of this, however, there emerged a unique and remarkable dialogue with the experience of this evil.[11] Each of us will almost certainly have encountered such courage and such nobility in the lives of others we have known. It is hard to see how such a spirit could emerge, except by rising to the challenge of extreme adversity. It is illuminating to see the truth of this spelt out by the pen of a poet. Edwin Muir, in his bleak but moving poem 'The Child Dying', writes thus:

> Unfriendly, friendly universe
> I pack your stars into my purse
> And bid you, bid you so farewell,
> That I can leave you, quite go out.
> Go out, go out beyond all doubt
> My father says, is the miracle . . .

Father, father, I dread this air
Blown from the far side of despair.
The cold, cold corner. What house, what hold,
What hand is there? I look and see
Nothing-filled eternity
And the great round world grows weak and old.[12]

Muir himself endured a bleak childhood, losing many of his siblings to tuberculosis. Even the religion of the Scottish islands where he was born and nurtured reinforced the sense of meaninglessness. Muir lost his Christian faith in his early twenties. Later, however, he began to see light in the darkness. Faith returned also. Elsewhere Muir picks up another, different note in what would be considered by some to be his best and indeed most perceptive poem. So in 'One Foot in Eden' he writes:

One foot in Eden still, I stand
And look across the other land.
The world's great day is growing late,
Yet strange these fields that we have planted
So long with crops of love and hate.

The poem ends:

But famished field and blackened tree
Bear flowers in Eden never known.
Blossoms of grief and charity
Bloom in these darkened fields alone.
What had Eden ever to say
Of hope and faith and pity and love
Until was buried all its day
And memory found its treasure trove?
Strange blessings never in Paradise
Fall from these beclouded skies.[13]
(Copyright © Willa Muir 1960)

Perhaps the most fascinating and encouraging point to emerge from this tiny snapshot of our encounter with the ambiguous nature of our world is its tendency to press us into asking deeper questions about meaning and purpose. The encounter with both darkness and beauty would leave only the coldest and most hardened heart untouched. At the very least we are challenged to reflect seriously on our lives, on the fact of our existence and upon all humanity making the best of the world in which it finds itself. But the Christian believer is pressed deeper still. For, despite the apparently negative signals of unjust suffering, despite the challenges represented by the cruelty of humans towards each other, we are driven back to ultimate questions about creation and redemption. The first and most remarkable question which the world presses upon us is the question – or better still, the experience – of grace. Why is there something rather than nothing? Why is there such unutterable beauty within creation? Why is Francis Kilvert made to cry out ecstatically at the joy of the world in which he finds himself? And then comes the obverse to that. Is the world and our experience of it any more explicable if we put down the dark clouds simply to meaninglessness? The extension of Mitchell's song at this point might not be simply 'not to let 'em know', but instead to assume the bleakest assumption of all – that the world has no meaning. Muir's first quoted poem seems to come close to that. His second poem, however, rejoices in the most noble responses of humanity to the bleaker parts of human experience. Dark and often meaningless as the experiences themselves may be, human transcendence of such tragedy and suffering points to a deeper sense of meaning which is somehow related to the existence of a Creator and Redeemer.

Christian experience down the centuries has not assumed that this individual response, either rejoicing at good or triumphing over evil, is the end of the story. The pattern of life and, in the face of death, the vindication of Jesus Christ is assuredly rooted in one individual. But the meaning and depth of that story reaches out into the whole of humanity. Even our own weakness can point us towards God. There, in the great hymn at Easter, the ancient *Exsultet*, we sing out '*O felix culpa*', O happy fault that won us so great a redeemer! It is this sort of reflection that gave birth to that pattern of life, thought, worship and prayer that we now describe as 'Christian theology'. It is that pattern too that helped countless generations of Christians to see the Church as acting as an instrument of God's grace in the world. Working with God our Creator, Sustainer and Redeemer, the Church acts as a channel of grace as God creates the Kingdom. The life, ministry, passion, death and resurrection of Jesus Christ is the unique and perfect living out of that in the world – here in Jesus, then, is the practical performative witness to that which the Church is called to live.

At this point our present chosen signature tune, from Joni Mitchell, begins to take on new resonances still. First of all, by reflecting on the world we have unavoidably found ourselves relating to God. So in a differing sense we find ourselves looking at 'both sides, now'. The message of the incarnation is that humanity and divinity are caught into a resonant unity and harmony in Jesus. Here that gracious gift of God is perfectly encountered; here that sense of gift which we experience in the world and in creation now permeates everything; here, to use the picture language of the gospel, earth and heaven become open to each other – we experience 'both sides, now'. There is still more to be said. One further gift in the incarnation is the willingness of God to become totally vulnerable by becoming human like us. We are now dealing with a quite different sort of God from that envisioned in some religious traditions. This is no god whose transcendence is so great that the deity is removed completely from human experience. That would be a god who would happily be described as one who would sign up to 'and if you care, don't let 'em know'. It would be a well-defended god, to use the modern jargon, a god where both sides – humanity and deity – remained sharply distanced from each other. Ours is a more daring, dangerous God, a God who gives selfhood away. Ours is a God who does not scorn the expense implied in the incarnation. W. H. Vanstone talks of *Love's Endeavour, Love's Expense*[14] – this is what God is about. God is there whenever the world stands on the brink of triumph and tragedy. That is where we are called to stand too.

So, then, we began unashamedly with the world, but the world has unavoidably taken us to God. In being taken to God, we receive back a challenge to live the life of Jesus Christ in the world. The Church too is called to stand wherever the world (in things both great and small) stands on the brink of triumph or tragedy; it is called in yet another sense to stand on 'both sides, now'. God and world are brought together whenever these vulnerabilities manifest themselves. Priests in God's Church are called to stand in this same place too. They stand on the *human side* of God and the *Godward side* of humanity. They do so by bearing witness at these moments of triumph and tragedy. Deacons and those called to the religious life bear witness too. Most obviously we see this in ministering to people as children are born and baptized, as lovers offer themselves to each other in the sacrament of marriage, and as individual people look over that other horizon towards death. These, and also countless other individual moments in people's lives, speak of triumph and/or of tragedy. But there are moments too when this relates to humanity more universally. It may relate to the great moral issues which we face continually. It may relate to matters of war and peace. One short vignette of a personal nature sets the scene here. Owen Chadwick, the distinguished professor of history, wrote movingly of his own experiences as a curate in Huddersfield in West Yorkshire, in the midst of the Second World War:

> On 31st October 1941, at breakfast time, more than fifty people were burnt to death in a factory fire in Yorkshire, and a few were killed when they jumped from the top storey down to the pavement. That was a long day. I spent most of it seeing burnt skin and the relatives of corpses, the most miserable day of my life.

But Chadwick continues:

> When at last I got home, after 11 p.m., dog-tired and empty and wretched, I opened a Bible and found, reluctantly, the lesson for the day. And the words leapt out from the page as though they were illuminated, and swept over my being like a metamorphosis, with relief and refreshment: 'The souls of the righteous are in the hands of God; and no torment shall touch them.'[15]

Chadwick here captures more than one element of priesthood. The sense of standing with tragedy is obvious, but the sense too of being with God, of being *both sides, now* is there vividly as he reflects upon that daily reading. The story points too to that way in which often a sense of crisis, by which we mean questioning and challenge, is part of the experience of both the priesthood of God's Church and of individual priests. That will become plain in the following chapter. Here too, however, Chadwick places this moment of great tragedy within the arms of God. We are drawn beyond individual tragedy to a sense of solidarity with all humanity, sadly often seen most vividly within war. Here we encounter, through such evil, the sin of the world. That stands out most sharply at the heart of the Eucharist just before the act of communion.

> O Lamb of God who takes away the sin of the world
> Have mercy upon us.

During the Falklands Conflict, the then chaplain to HMS *Hermes* was in the midst of presiding at the Eucharist when the 'action stations' sounded at just this point, as people were saying the *Agnus Dei*, 'O Lamb of God'. Everyone scattered to their positions on different parts of the ship and the eucharistic vessels were put away safely. At the end of the air raid, much to the priest's surprise, all returned to complete the Eucharist: never, he reflected, never before had those words about the 'sin of the world' spoken to him so vividly. So there we see the world, the Church and the individual minister coming together within the Eucharist. There too we see vividly a conjoining of the individual and humanity in solidarity. It is the sin of the world for which forgiveness is being asked, even though each individual is aware of his or her part in that broader distortion of our humanity. Both sides are there. Here priesthood is sharply defined. Priests and deacons and other ministers stand as representative of all humanity and also do so in relation to God. At that very same moment they are standing with God representing God to all humanity. Michael Ramsey described this lyrically in his reflections which came to be *The Christian Priest Today*. One significant shift since the writing of that book has been the decision by the General Synod of the Church of England to ordain women as well as men to the priesthood. There remains a substantial group within the Church of England which believes this decision to have been a mistake. There are now therefore two streams within Anglicanism in England. This book is written for people within both those different streams, with the belief that the basic theological thrust which stands behind its argument is shared by the whole Church and is focused in the individual ministry of all ordained ministers within that Church. This does not, of course, ignore some specific points of disagreement in relation to the historical tradition and the possibility of ordaining both men and women as part of that tradition.

Assuming, however, that the main thrust of the argument for a representative ministry is held in common more widely with Anglicanism, this last piece of discussion, originating within the context of the Falklands War, takes us to the heart of the representative nature of both God's Church and individual ministers within that Church. It is frequently at times of crisis, either in individual lives or within the wider world, that the nature of priesthood becomes sharply focused. We have reflected upon the world and its ambiguities; we have from within those ambiguities encountered questions about God and the world. What is it about a world in crisis, often seen through the lives of individual people or in the broader context, that engages humanity with the really serious questions about meaning and purpose? It is to those questions provoked by a world in crisis that we now turn.

2

American pie

The world in crisis

————◦•◦————

I can't remember if I cried
When I read about his widowed bride,
But something touched me deep inside
The day the music died.[1]

'American pie' belongs to the 1970s rather than the 1960s, although Don McLean wrote it in the late 1960s. It became almost iconic for a certain period, and perhaps the key line in the song is the last one quoted above. Indeed, if we had not been using song titles to head our chapters, we might have called this section 'The day the music died'. For many, excellent as the beat may be, the song is rambling. But that line offers the key, for it refers to the death in an air crash of Buddy Holly, the American popular rock singer. On his death Holly became overnight a symbol of the rock and roll era and a number of his songs became 'all time favourites'. But why was his death significant to McLean? Was it really as significant as the cryptic lyrics suggest? The answer is a qualified yes. For McLean remarks that the death of Buddy Holly in 1959 marked the beginning of his transition from light – that is, the innocence of childhood – to darkness – that is, the darker realities of adulthood. McLean further reflects that this transition period reached its conclusion with the assassination of President John F. Kennedy in 1963. During that four-year spell McLean moved from a fairly idyllic childhood through the harsh and dark realities of his father's death in 1961 to his decision to pack up his university career and pursue his dream to become a professional singer in 1963.

So there is an autobiographical element in the origin of the song, which also resonates with the collapse of the more optimistic and lighter mood of the early 1960s into the darkness of the late years of the decade. The lyrics of the song are fascinating:

Did you write the book of love,
And do you have faith in God above,
If the Bible tells you so?
Do you believe in rock 'n' roll,
Can music save your mortal soul,
And can you teach me how to dance real slow?

The fears of a darker age are played out:

Helter skelter in a summer swelter.
The birds flew off with a fallout shelter,
Eight miles high and falling fast.

Later still the lyrics become still more 'off the wall':

Oh, and there we were all in one place,
A generation lost in space,
With no time left to start again.
So come on: Jack be nimble, Jack be quick,
Jack Flash sat on a candlestick,
'Cos fire is the devil's only friend.

Space prohibits further quotation, but if you didn't know the song to start with, you are probably beginning to get the idea, especially if you imagine it moving to a catchy and fast-moving rhythm. Predictably such enigmatic but sometimes high-sounding – almost metaphysical – thoughts have prompted 30 years of analysis. The research continues and people still search for the song's *real* meaning. All of this stands against the backcloth of McLean never talking about the song and never offering to give others an insight into what the lyrics are about. There is enough there, however, to capture the imagination of later generations trying to make sense of a period overshadowed by the threat of nuclear war; of a visionary time shattered by the deaths of the youthful John Kennedy, Bobby Kennedy and Martin Luther King; and of a period of LSD and flower-power culminating in the murder of John Lennon. Lennon also gets a mention in the song though, of course, his death would follow later.

Such lyrics, when attached to a legendary period or person, exert a fatal fascination. It has always been so. Indeed, in the early nineteenth century, Samuel Taylor Coleridge's *The Rime of the Ancient Mariner* had an equal effect on a very different generation. Coleridge, a writer and philosopher of genius, the son of an Anglican clergyman, would be a living paradox. Committed to Christian belief throughout his life, he would handle his marriage and home life appallingly. One of the most creative poets and philosophers of his age, he would punish his body with increasing opium abuse. Coleridge was not unaware of his fallibility and part of the energy behind the generation of his great work doubtless issued from his sense of his own flawed life and the mysterious origins of sin and evil. So, in the poem, the killing of the albatross, which was hung round the mariner's neck, tells its own story. At the time, however, readers and critics were irritated by the impenetrability of the verses. One recent commentator reflects that there was a repeated demand for the poem to be clear to the understanding and to carry a definable message.[2] In the *Monthly Review* for June 1799, the following ambivalent, semi-hostile review noted:

> [*The Ancient Mariner*] is the strangest story of a cock and a bull that we ever saw on paper: yet, though it seems a rhapsody of unintelligible wildness and incoherence, (of which we do not perceive the drift, unless the joke lies in depriving the wedding guest of his share of the feast) there are in it poetical touches of an exquisite kind.[3]

For all its complexity and apparent impenetrability, the sentiments just three stanzas from the end are almost naïve:

> He prayeth best, who loveth best
> All things both great and small;
> For the dear God who loveth us,
> He made and loveth all.[4]

So, then, for all their hyperbole and apparently deliberate incomprehensibility, both of these pieces from the nineteenth and twentieth centuries – Coleridge's *Ancient Mariner* and McLean's 'American pie' – despite their very different intellectual and cultural depths pinpoint one key issue for us. The issue is this: it is often when either our own world is in crisis, or the world in general finds itself in upheaval, that serious questions of meaning and purpose are asked. Furthermore, in finding ourselves interrogated by our experience in this way, we are also made to ask how we should respond to the dilemmas and crises of our world. To use a term much favoured a generation ago, existential crises can be the most effective provokers of really serious engagement with our world. Dag Hammarskjöld, arguably the most intellectually and spiritually serious Secretary General of the United Nations to date, saw this very clearly. As he flew all over the world seeking to bring reconciliation and peace, in crisis after crisis, within nation after nation across the world, he reflected sharply not just on his work, but on the human condition. His spiritual notebook, *Markings*, is peppered with wisdom and seriousness about the world and its crises, and about the challenge to us as individuals and to the human race. So he wrote at one point:

> Pray that your loneliness may spur you into finding something to live for, great enough to die for.[5]

A highly religious man himself, Hammarskjöld exercised a sort of secular priestly role on behalf of the community of nations and thus ultimately on behalf of humanity. Eventually, he did so to the extent of effectively becoming a martyr, not necessarily on account of a criminal assassination, but certainly through his willingness to give everything on behalf of his fellow men and women. He died in a plane crash while seeking to bring peace in the Congo. Hammarskjöld, of course, lived a most unusual life, jetting across the world and being constantly entangled in international politics at the highest level. This is hardly typical of most of our lives. Nevertheless, that sense of crisis, challenge and urgency is something which all of us encounter. Sometimes it will be an individual personal crisis; McLean describes that in the premature death of his father. Sometimes the crisis will be of universal or near-universal significance. A brief glance over one's shoulder back into fairly recent history indicates the effects of such epoch-making events.

The classic example has already been mentioned. Almost everyone who was around at the time can remember what they were doing when the news of John Kennedy's assassination came through. I was at school, waiting for a careers evening to begin; my parents were with me. The head teacher began the meeting in sombre tones, explaining that President Kennedy had been shot. It was not until later that it was confirmed that he had been mortally wounded. The effects of Kennedy's death have still, to some extent, not entirely disappeared. Here was a young, handsome and eloquent president who represented hope for the future. Kennedy was one of the key emblems of the 1960s, standing alongside the elderly but invigorating Pope John XXIII, who had set in train the Second Vatican Council. Then there were the Beatles, who had helped wrest the laurel wreath of popular music from the western side of the Atlantic

Ocean to bring it to the British Isles. It was the decade of Andy Warhol's pop art where Campbell's soup cans replaced the Madonna and Child; it was the decade which ushered in David Hockney's new artistic realism. There were myriad others too in both high and popular culture. Intellectually the world seemed to be buzzing with new ideas. In theology too this was true. On the western side of the Atlantic Harvey Cox celebrated the 'secular city'. Over on the eastern side of the ocean, the 'old world' throbbed to the rhythm of 'South Bank theology'; Bishop John Robinson's *Honest to God* was the trademark of this, at least within England. It was a theological approach which sought to engage with the world. Its critics believed that it had effectively sold out to the world.

Kennedy's death, then, cut at the roots of this new-found confidence. Arguably it also redrew the map of American politics, which would be further scarred by the Watergate crisis and the threat of Richard Nixon's impeachment in the 1970s. An entire generation was sent into shock through the news of the President's death. Furthermore, American confidence in its own pioneering dream was to be battered twice more. The murder of Bobby Kennedy, the late President's brother (and another star), and then the assassination too of Martin Luther King added to that sense of nightmare. Since the USA was now one of only two world superpowers and the flag carrier for anti-Soviet Western democracy, the effects of all these tragedies struck at the heart of Western self-consciousness. 'American pie' encapsulates both the remarkable hope which had dawned and the cruel dashing of these hopes.

There was more, however, which presented a feeling of crisis and challenge:

> Helter skelter in a summer swelter
> The birds flew off with a fallout shelter.[6]

Throughout the 1950s and 1960s an entire generation grew up under the shadow of possible instant annihilation through the development of the hydrogen bomb and ICBMs (inter-continental ballistic missiles). Driving up the A1 Great North Road in the 1960s you would pass RAF Woolfox. Set out there on the tarmac of a World War II aerodrome were a great number of *Bloodhound* anti-aircraft missiles, all facing east, ready to intercept the expected Soviet threat – or at the very least to bluff the enemy into keeping the peace through the strategy of mutually assured destruction, suitably shortened to MAD. In 1962 this all came into closer focus with the Cuban Missile Crisis. President Khrushchev surreptitiously decided that the Soviet Union would supply Fidel Castro with nuclear missiles to sit on America's very doorstep! Kennedy, in consultation with Harold Macmillan, the British Prime Minister, set up a blockade in defiance of Khrushchev's threat. In the nick of time, the Russian ships turned back; Macmillan had already moved the British *Thor* nuclear missiles into a state of immediate readiness. I can well remember sitting in class for an economics lesson. As the teacher droned on about the functions of the central bank, I can remember reflecting: 'All this is a waste of our time; this time next week, "the old lady of Threadneedle Street", the Bank of England, will, as likely as not, be part of one vast nuclear cloud blowing its way around our dead planet.'

Small wonder, then, that the assassination of John Kennedy had such a traumatic effect after which the USA's confident self-image would never be quite the same again. Small wonder, too, that in any number of different ways the 1960s would drive forward countless people to offer a myriad of different ideological, philosophical and theological responses to what was perceived as 'humanity in crisis'. Some argued for an atheistic vision which nevertheless would underpin a new humanism; socialism's self-confidence had not yet been punctured by the collapse of the Soviet ideological dream. The Berlin Wall was a potent symbol of Russian defiance. More positively for believers there would issue any number of different theological responses. From the secularizing theologians would come 'Death of God theology' – now consigned to an entry in theological reference books. From Joseph Fletcher and John Robinson would arise 'the new morality'. Daniel Berrigan and others would offer a new vision of political theology; the first stirrings of liberation theology were also emerging, especially following the Second Vatican Council. Finally, at the very end of the 1960s, Peter Berger would write *A Rumour of Angels*.[7] Was God re-emerging from the end of a dark tunnel?

All this, then, left its mark upon the Church in a most stimulating way. The great Second Ecumenical Council held at the Vatican in Rome, now under the presidency of a new pope, Paul VI, would focus sharply upon the vocation of God's Church. It would do so in a manner where not one stone was left unturned. The documents of Vatican II remain a deposit of enormous richness almost half a century later. Indeed, they will doubtless take their place as milestones in the development of the Christian tradition over the centuries. Declarations on the liturgy, on the nature of the Church and on the Church's mission in the world all offered together an integrated vision of the way in which the Church is now called to live out the life which God makes plain through the incarnation, in Jesus Christ. Alongside these documents, the decree on ecumenism, *Unitatis Redintegratio*, for the first time since the Reformation, saw the Roman Catholic Church looking out to the other churches in sisterly love. The Ecumenical Movement, which traced its roots back to the 1910 Edinburgh international conference on mission, had been the vanguard of ecumenical enterprise. It allowed other churches to respond to the overtures both implied and made explicit in Vatican II's new outward-facing stance. Now, through the World Council of Churches, the Faith and Order Commission and the Pontifical Council for Promoting Christian Unity (as it became) at the Vatican, the vocation of God's Church could be looked at afresh by different churches together with other Christian bodies – including, for example, the Religious Society of Friends (Quakers) and the Salvation Army.

For all the uncertainties of the 1960s, there was a new sense of energy and resourcefulness which led in some churches to a boost in individuals offering themselves for the priesthood and other forms of ministry. It was the mid-late 1960s, then, which saw a great flowering of vocations within the Anglican Franciscan movement. What had been a fairly tiny but determined group of friars (formed by the merger of two smaller groups between the wars) burst forth and became an international Society of St Francis. Eventually, there would be some 200 or so members living in community, in three different orders. In due course there would also be more than 2,000 members of the Third Order, living a Franciscan rule within the wider world. What had provoked in these idealistic young people such a radical response? It was simply that that emphasis of Francis' own witness and example spoke sharply to this generation.

The radical challenges of the early thirteenth century spoke to the equally clear challenge of the twentieth. 'Rebuild my Church,' Francis had heard God say to him through Jesus on the cross in the Church of San Damiano, just on the edge of Assisi. So Francis duly set about rebuilding it, both literally and metaphorically. Starting with the tiny ruined Church of the Portiuncola (the Little Portion) near Assisi, he and a band of friends made it once again a suitable place for prayer and eucharist. More dramatically he gave up a comfortable life – he was the son of a prosperous cloth merchant – and set up as a mendicant friar, that is living on what people gave him to survive. Others joined him and by the time of his death in 1226, at the age of only 43, there were thousands of these *poverellos* (little poor men) all over Europe. The friars arrived in England, all the way across mediaeval Europe, some three years before Francis himself died. Francis helped his friend Clare to set up a contemplative community – the Second Order – also committed to the life of poverty, after the manner of their Saviour, Jesus Christ.

It was this vision, then, that encouraged those considerable numbers of both women and men to offer for the active and contemplative life in the Society of St Francis and the Community of St Clare, spurred on by the new sense of vision in the 1960s. Both societies continue to witness to the vocation of all Christians throughout the world. Also in 1968, to offer one other slightly different example, there was born the Community of Sant'Egidio in Rome. In this case, with the encouragement of Pope Paul VI, a small number of professionals – some still students then – committed themselves to a lay life of Christian prayer and action. This too had a Franciscan flavour. Andrea Riccardi, its founder, and his associates took over the tiny church of Sant'Egidio in Trastevere on the left bank of the River Tiber in Rome and started an evening prayer service. Alongside this, the members of the community offered their time generously in Christian social work and witness. The Roman daily work pattern commends itself better to this than the longer working days of northern Europe. Many people begin their work very early and end at siesta time at 1.30 or 2 p.m. Thereafter members of the community commit their time to helping the poor. Now there are some 15,000 members of the community in Italy alone and perhaps 45,000 world-wide. The work to which they are committed is very varied. Packing up food parcels for the homeless in Rome has led to extensive work with illegal immigrants (notably from North Africa); there is now a 'soup kitchen' or cafeteria offering free meals to immigrants, and above this is a language school. Nearby is a hostel for children born with AIDS, opened by Archbishop Desmond Tutu in the late 1980s. It was the Community of Sant'Egidio too which brokered the peace which ended the civil war in Mozambique. More recently it looks as if a lasting peace may have been brokered by members of the same community working in Uganda.

Out of crises and challenges, then, issued a new sense of vocation for God's Church, and out of this also there often issued an offering by people of their lives – in many different ways – to work with the Church in pursuing that vocation. The story of such crises did not begin nor indeed end, of course, in the 1960s. In 1997, the tragic death of Princess Diana was again one of those defining moments when all can remember where they were when the news broke. This time, for those of us living in England, the news came at the break of the day. I was set to preach at a country church in Norfolk. My sermon, I realized, was useless; I would have done better to have suggested ten minutes of silent prayer. We were all caught completely unprepared – not only by the dreadful news itself, but by the unique way in which the nation (and even to some degree the world) responded. This time the churches, and perhaps most generally the Church of England through its parish churches and cathedrals, found itself as one of the focuses of the crisis. Condolence books, candle pricket stands and open churches are the prevailing memory of those extraordinary days. Countless people came into church buildings to light a candle, to pray, to sit in silence or simply 'to weep with those who weep'. Ten years on and it is still not clear how the Church did (or indeed, better still, ought to) respond to those events. There is no doubt that people needed the Church – or at least churches. There is also no doubt that in many places individual priests, deacons, religious and lay people responded heroically. But there was still a feeling that Elton John's 'Candle in the wind' caught the mood of the moment more than did some of the official responses of the Church and its leaders. Nonetheless, respond the Church did, and there remains an agenda to be pursued. How does the vocation of the Church need further to mutate in order to speak to such moments?

Something similar, if less dramatic, happened to the Church in the aftermath of the devastating attacks on the twin towers in New York on September 11, 2001. This time the churches were a little clearer about how they needed to respond. In New York, St Paul's Church, next door to the scene of devastation, acted as the base for all who ministered to the dying and bereaved. In the UK, churches again became the depositories for flowers and condolences. In this case, a further complexity presented itself inasmuch as the crisis itself was borne of religion, albeit not the Christian religion. Perhaps there should be one more reflection, issuing from this last point, on 'crises and challenges' before we move on.

On 7 July 2005, four individual bombs were detonated by Islamic extremists on the London underground and on a bus. By an amazing irony that same day also saw the Archbishop of Canterbury travelling to West Yorkshire to meet with Muslim leaders. He had come to enter dialogue with those leaders and to see how such dialogue might both enrich our religious witness and also engender greater community coherence. It was a remarkable occasion. As the truth of the situation unfolded the Archbishop realized that he would have to comment. He did so outside the National Coal Mining Museum, close to Horbury. The museum is itself a clear symbol of the formerly predominantly white indigenous industrial culture of that part of England; the fact that he spoke outside a *museum*, where his meetings would continue, pressed home the contrast between a culture now past and a new culture existing. The ironies of that day were further to emerge in the days ahead when it became clear that the main strategist among the suicide bombers came from Thornhill Lees, but three miles or so from the museum, and on the route which the Archbishop had taken earlier that day. Here, then, lay the roots of yet another challenge to God's Church to review how it lives out its vocation in a multi-racial and multi-cultural world. This is certainly not to argue for some form of inter-faith accommodation – what is often described as syncretism. Instead we are prompted to review again how the Church lives out its vocation and how ordained ministers, in such multi-racial contexts, remain confident in the gospel yet also sensitive to the other religious traditions which prevail.

This chapter, then, has been looking at the world and seeing how crises and epoch-making events challenge both the self-consciousness of societies and also the way in which the Church understands its vocation. How should the Church respond anew to such a changed self-consciousness? But moving on from some of the bleaker moments in contemporary history, there have also been some similarly remarkable changes for good, moments of insight and positively critical moments. On what might we focus here? Having noted earlier the tragedy of Martin Luther King's assassination, we have so far passed over in silence the positive contribution made by King in his own life and witness. There can be hardly a school now in the United Kingdom, let alone in the rest of the world, that does not include a lesson, an assembly or even a project on the work of Martin Luther King. Ironically again, his tragic death reinforced and immortalized the significance of his witness. His speech 'I have a dream . . .' has now become a classic statement within the canon of modern literature. The seeds of Martin Luther King's witness lie, of course, in the Christian gospel. This he lived out, within the vocation of his own particular Christian tradition. He saw it as an integral part of the vocation of the whole of God's Church, fragmented as that Church is.

Other events have been equally positive, even when they have issued from tragic circumstances. The television footage shot in Ethiopia by the BBC and the commentary which accompanied it, led by Michael Buerk and Mike Wooldridge, did nothing less than transform Western attitudes to the terrible suffering through war and famine in developing countries. The policy of the USA towards international aid was radically changed through the effects of these broadcasts on human consciousness internationally. Similarly the work of Bob Geldof and the Live Aid concerts, and all that has followed since, issued from the power of these broadcasts and the terrifying scenes which they communicated and indeed brought into the living rooms of people across Europe and North

America. This transformation is to be celebrated, and Christian people and churches played a key role in all this.

In a rather different manner, the amazing events of 1989, with the final collapse of the Soviet Empire and the breaching of the Berlin Wall, opened up to the world possibilities that hitherto could not have been imagined. Tragically these changes would also lead to instability, terrible bloodshed and ethnic cleansing in the countries of the former Yugoslavia. But the ultimate possibility of a reunited, more just and peaceful Europe is also beginning to emerge. Here, it was the churches which had retained a visionary and prophetic stance ever since the end of the Second World War. The Conference of European Churches, which includes Orthodox, Reformed, Lutheran, Anglican and other groups, refused to recognize the Iron Curtain. Similarly, the grouping which brings together Roman Catholic Bishops' Conferences from across the whole of Europe, known as the CCEE, refused to accept the divisions implied by the Iron Curtain. These prophetic stances were part of the Church living out its vocation in the world in a time of dire international division and tension.

One final example here must be the final defeat of apartheid in South Africa. There is no denying the political nature of this defeat and the significance of South Africa's increasing isolation from the international community. This isolation was accompanied by a similar isolation and squeeze upon South Africa's economy. Nevertheless, at the centre of the nation's own fight for racial equality stood the outstanding witness of the Christian Church. This included Reformed Church leaders including Dr Beyers Naudé. It included a sustained witness from Roman Catholics, but it also, and perhaps most charismatically, involved the work of a number of Anglicans. Pre-eminent among Anglican church leaders was Desmond Tutu, not only as Secretary of the South African Council of Churches and later Archbishop of Cape Town, but also later on as the Chair of the Truth and Reconciliation Commission. Tutu, inspired by the example of Father Trevor Huddleston and Bishops Ambrose Reeves and Joost de Blank, and supported by countless others, discerned very clearly one specific aspect of the vocation of the Church of God in South Africa. The remarkable leadership of Nelson Mandela and his extra-ordinarily conciliatory response following his release from Robben Island and election as president all once again traced their roots to the Christian gospel. This brings us fortuitously to the concluding section of this chapter.

Clarifying and pursuing the vocation of the Church and the Christian life often issues from the belief that the world can and ought to be a better place. As a young man I toyed with the thought of entering politics.

My father had been an active local politician and the adrenalin which electiontide squirted into the blood left its mark on me in my childhood, sitting taking people's voting numbers, as I did outside polling stations from the age of ten onwards. As I matured, and indeed as I returned to an active Christian faith, I changed my mind. The broader and deeper vision of the Christian gospel caught hold of my being. The world could (and should) indeed be a better place, and God in Jesus Christ offers a vision which embraces, but goes beyond, a social and political vision. The mission of God and of God's Church is rooted in prayer and worship and thus embraces the spiritual. Spirituality here does not refer to that vague and very broad spectrum brought together in the 'Mind and Spirit' sections of contemporary bookshops. It is instead rooted in the spirituality of and belief in the God of Jesus Christ. The social and political vision are then part of that long stream which we call the Judaeo-Christian tradition. In this tradition, belief in God cannot be separated from the vision of a transformed world. So it was that, as my heart and mind were shifting towards a more committed belief, books like Trevor Huddleston's *Naught for Your Comfort*[8] and *Cry, the Beloved Country*[9] by Alan Paton (a South African Anglican lay person) touched my human spirit, anointing it with the spirit of God. Huddleston's book is prefixed with a quotation from G. K. Chesterton's poem 'The Ballad of the White Horse' which runs:

> I tell you naught for your comfort,
> Yea, naught for your desire
> Save that the sky grows darker yet
> And the sea rises higher.

Here then is the origin of Huddleston's title, and herein too is demonstrated his passion that things could and must be different in South Africa. The narrative of Huddleston's account of the situation in the suburb of Sophiatown in Johannesburg and of his ministry there make it abundantly clear that such change issues as an imperative from the Christian gospel. It is there too in the Old Testament; another chapter is prefaced with a verse from Isaiah:

> Woe unto them that join house to house, that lay field to field, till there be no place.[10]

Paton, too, in a book which comes as close to being poetry as it does to being a novel, captures the tragedy of apartheid in South Africa and the way in which it undermined and poisoned the human spirit:

Cry, the beloved country, for the unborn child that is the inheritor
of our fear. Let him not love the earth too deeply . . . For fear will
rob him of all if he gives too much.[11]

There, then, within just one individual lie the seeds which provoked an
offering of something of one's life in the hope that it might help further
the vocation of God's Church in the world, of realizing the gospel of
Jesus Christ in the world in which we find ourselves. This has been put
far more powerfully by others. The present Archbishop of Canterbury,
Dr Rowan Williams, has reflected simply: 'Are not Christian people those
who believe that things could be different?' That difference, he goes
on to explain, resides in the life and ministry, passion and resurrection
of Jesus Christ. Again, most eloquently, Professor Sam Wells captured
it when addressing a congregation on Vocation Sunday in Norwich
Cathedral some years ago. There is space here only to include his conclusion, which springs from a sermon that begins by asking his listeners:
'What do you want? What do you really, really want?' Wells then offers
some attractive possibilities – a Guinness glass that everlastingly refills
itself; the possibility of being a world-class footballer. Then, in an imaginary interview with St Peter, the issue of wants is taken deeper. We move
from what we want to what we need. We need *leaders* who will somehow
help others see what God is like and how the world might come to live
more in God's image. Wells ends thus:

> When you hold up your hands to receive God's gift, will you be
> saying, 'Please, God, I want some more?' Do you want more? Do
> you really, really want more? Do you want more wonder, more
> faith, more love? Do you want more life, more depth, more joy?
> Do you want to be part of the solution? Do you want to be a
> priest?[12]

*　　*　　*

We began with a world in crisis, but we have touched too upon a world
in celebration and transformation. In all of this we have also touched
upon how such crisis alerts humanity to respond. It shifts humanity's
self-consciousness. It challenges the Church too to reflect on its vocation
and on how individual Christians can do the same. Towards the end of
his song McLean writes:

> And in the streets: the children screamed,
> The lovers cried, and the poets dreamed.

But not a word was spoken.
The church bells all were broken
And the three men I admire most:
The father, son and holy ghost
They caught the last train for the coast
The day the music died!

That is where we depart from McLean's song. For our conclusion has been that, despite the crises of the world, the music has not died. We can still sing the Lord's song, even if it does feel as if we are doing it in a strange land. Sam Wells talks of more faith, more love, more life, more depth, more joy. Certainly, in the face of so many crises all these have poured forth. The Christian believes that this has only been possible through the grace of God. For the puzzles and even apparently meaningless things of our world can lead to Wells' sixth gift – more wonder. The sheer fact of us being here at all provokes this. Philosopher Ludwig Wittgenstein wrote:

It is not how the world is but that it is that is the mystical.[13]

So the mystical and indeed the mystery of God are provoked by even the most worldly reflections. Albert Einstein wrote:

The fairest thing we can experience is the mysterious. It is the fundamental emotion which stands at the cradle of true art and true science. He who knows it not and can no longer wonder, no longer feel amazement, is as good as dead, a snuffed-out candle. It was the experience of mystery – even if mixed with fun – that engendered religion. A knowledge of the existence of something we cannot penetrate, of the manifestations of the profoundest reason and the most radiant beauty which are only accessible to our reason in their most elementary forms – it is this knowledge and this emotion that constitute the truly religious attitude; in this sense, and in this alone, I am a deeply religious man.[14]

For the Christian it is no distance at all from here to God, and it is God who now fully enters upon our scene . . .

3

Imagine

God

————◆•◆◆————

Imagine there's no Heaven
It's easy if you try
No hell below us
Above us only sky
Imagine all the people
Living for today.[1]

In some ways, John Lennon's 'Imagine' captured the feel of the late 1960s perfectly. It was a song which prompted the hearer to a broader and fresher vision. Casting off the mantle of tradition and the straitjacket of convention it envisaged a fresh new world epitomized in those final lines: 'Imagine all the people/Living for today.' The rest of the song fleshes out more of that liberated imaginative world, where all of those constraints which bind us into war, starvation and oppression are removed. First it touches upon our humanity hemmed in, imprisoned and doomed to conflict by the nation-state:

> Imagine there's no countries
> It isn't hard to do
> Nothing to kill or die for.

Forty years later and things do not feel that different. Conflict in the Middle East seems to have become an unavoidable part of the reality of our world. Not only that, but it is undoubtedly the 'countries' which fuel the war and terrorism. It is not only the state of Israel, born of the Balfour Declaration in the early twentieth century and claiming its own nationhood from the British mandate just after the Second World War. It is also the other Arab nations carved out of the old Ottoman Empire often by drawing arbitrary lines on a map. So these manufactured nations brought with them their own political problems and inner tensions.

But those arbitrary lines were also drawn by other countries – the Allied powers themselves had had their imperial pretensions and these too brought with them their own hints of struggles for power. Much of this focuses on what has become known as 'the Holy Land' – that is, the land where Jesus walked, ministered and spoke of God. More complicated still, Jerusalem, standing at the heart of all these disputed territories, is a focus for three of the world's great religions – Judaism, Christianity and Islam. Small wonder conflict remains the order of the day – and so to Lennon's next lines:

> . . . and no religion too
> Imagine all the people
> Living life in peace.

Here the situation is very different from the 1960s, a decade which celebrated secularization and in doing so effectively appeared to welcome the increasing marginal nature of religion. Now, religion's importance can hardly be overplayed, and often 'furious religion' at that. The conflicts continue and often are caught up with religion. Such was the case in the 1990s in Bosnia, and such has been the case more recently in Afghanistan. The sentiments of Lennon's verse may be easier to understand now, but more difficult to *imagine*, within a world which is largely more driven by religion. Lennon, however, was describing a vision which went well beyond religions and political liberation. It was a vision of humanity untrammelled by all the restrictive conventions of the past. It was a world of free love where each individual could make up his or her own mind about the way life would unfold. Indeed, much of what he describes has an undoubted nobility and virtue issuing from it. Look at his last two verses:

> Imagine no possessions
> I wonder if you can
> No need for greed or hunger
> A brotherhood of man
> Imagine all the people
> Sharing all the world.
>
> You may say that I'm a dreamer
> But I'm not the only one
> I hope someday you'll join us
> And the world will live as one.

Ignoring the dated lyrics which speak exclusively of 'a brotherhood of man', the song's vision is tempting for any of us. Furthermore it has much in common with that older and apparently more constrained world. Think back from a moment to our previous chapter and the life and witness of Francis of Assisi. Francis and his friends lived in brotherhoods and sisterhoods where all was held in common – indeed, where very little was 'held' at all. They lived on what others gave them and they had already disavailed themselves of all possessions. The Franciscan vision was one which reclaimed the teaching of Jesus where his followers were challenged to give away all that they had and follow him. Jesus' teaching, and indeed the life he lived and the death he died, also reflected something of Lennon's first verse. He talks of 'imagining all the people living for today'. That does not sound wildly different from the words of Jesus as reported in the Gospel according to St Matthew.

> Therefore do not be anxious about tomorrow, for tomorrow will be anxious for itself. Let the day's own trouble be sufficient for the day.[2]

Is not 'living for the day' precisely the same as 'not being anxious about tomorrow'? Are they not saying just the same thing? Or are they? First of all, Jesus is not somehow implying that 'the day' – the present – is all that we should bother with. There is more to it than that, 'for tomorrow will be anxious for itself' and so each day will bring its trials, concerns and moral claims. There is, of course, another more significant contrast in these two sets of attitudes. Jesus sets this piece of teaching in the midst of what we now call 'the sermon on the mount'. That sermon begins with that lyrical description of life in God known as the beatitudes. Chapter 5, which begins with the beatitudes, ends with the verse:

> You, therefore, must be perfect, as your heavenly Father is perfect.[3]

Matthew's next chapter, with its reflection about tomorrow, enlarges on this teaching with a series of sayings which help fill out what living the life of God might mean. Lennon's vision is very different: 'Imagine there's no heaven . . . no hell below us, above us only sky . . . Imagine there's no countries . . . And no religion too . . .' Although God does not get a mention, all the implications are clear – Lennon's world is a world without God, and the assumption seems to be that it will be all the better for that.

Yet remembering the apparent similarity of the viewpoints which we have outlined, would it really make any difference if we did without God? Admittedly the crises of our world in the last chapter seemed to engage us with God, but does it really matter? After all, John Lennon's verses included a plentiful sense of altruism. People would be living in peace with nothing to kill or die for. The world would be as one, with no greed or hunger and with humanity sharing all that there is within the world. This seems to mirror much of the altruism of Francis' little poor ones; it stands close to some of the teaching in the beatitudes. Certainly there have been visions of the world which entirely exclude God but where 'things are different', to pick up those challenges from the end of the previous chapter. Some of these visions have been lived out in the past two centuries and it is worth reflecting for a moment on what they had to offer.

One of the earliest of these visions in the modern era was that which seemed to spark off the French Revolution. Apart from the weak government and lack of direction which preceded the events of 1789, there was, as the revolution began, a clear moral purpose at its heart. This was encapsulated in the phrase that became the motto or war cry of the revolution: *Liberté, Egalité, Fraternité*. Translated into the modern idiom one might restyle this as liberty, fraternity and the solidarity of all of us in one humanity. It was, of course, entangled with a revival of French nationalism superbly captured in the 'Marseillaise', which indeed became the national anthem. It is no accident that once the antinomian impulse of the revolution had run its course France slipped into the Napoleonic period of totalitarian aggression. By this time the nation was in desperate need of clear leadership and a sense of purpose. The first years of the revolution, culminating in 1794 in the Vendée, were effectively a time of continuous upheaval. Within the ruling cabal there would be almost constant perfidy. The bloodletting within the incessantly changing régime was shocking in itself, but this too led to an apparent dismissal of the significance of the loss of life even on a grand scale. The massacres in western France during the period of the Vendée were dire and of tragic proportions. Nevertheless, some in England were prepared to go along with this simply because of the vision of freedom which seemed to energize the revolution. So Charles James Fox spoke enthusiastically for the revolution. After the fall of the Bastille, Fox wrote of the revolution: 'How much the greatest event it is that has ever happened in the world and how much the best![4] Tom Paine too had written critically of the negative reaction of Edmund Burke to the revolution: 'he pities the plumage and forgets the dying bird'. Paine clearly thought that the liberty obtained was worth some bloodshed.

Paine's comment is crucial since it takes us to the heart of a world without God. Edmund Burke had, after all, always been on the side of freedom. He was almost a radical – certainly a campaigner – over India, Ireland and North America. The revolution in France, however, saw Burke taking a quite different stance on issues of liberty and of how liberty should be achieved. So he wrote:

> Men must have a certain fund of natural moderation to qualify them for Freedom, else it become noxious to themselves and a perfect nuisance to everybody else.[5]

At the heart of Burke's apparent shift from a universal support for egalitarianism to a more conservative approach lay the issue of morality and religion. Burke had been moved to write his *Reflections on the Revolution in France* as early as 1791; his argument on the likely outcome of the rebellion was prophetic; the Vendée at that point still lay three years into the future. Burke saw, however, that the deliberately anti-Catholic and atheistic trends within the revolutionary régime would divorce morality from any objective base. The politics of the state, even when they were agreed to issue from an ethical root, would now be entirely positivistic: so an individual or a group could derive their or its own morality without reference to any external authority. Burke was a significant influence upon the government in England. Even when William Pitt was less than enthusiastic about continuing the war with France, it was arguments like those rehearsed here that convinced the Prime Minister that he must remain resolute. Pitt was not greatly taken by religion, but the moral heartlessness of a humanity without God still horrified him and made him fearful for the future of his own nation.[6] Effectively this meant that there was nothing necessarily that lay 'off limits'. This vacuum at the heart of the state, this amorality, allowed the terrible massacres of the Vendée to take place. It also allowed for the collapse of stable government. When Napoleon showed himself to be a great military leader, he was also able to assume the reigns of power and give stability back to the nation. Furthermore, the advent of the revolution meant that he took over a state with an extreme level of central control and where morality was also decided by the state.

The French Revolution was effectively the first ever experiment within a nation in God being removed from the equation and it had devastating effects upon the received view of the dignity of humanity.

This is not necessarily to argue that morality and religion are logically inseparable. It is, however, to suggest that removing God from the equation does drastically affect society's view of itself.

We have spent some time reflecting on the French Revolution since it was effectively a turning point in modern history with regard to God, the Church, morality and the state. The anti-clericalism which it ignited in France has never since been quenched. More significant still, the experience and effects of the revolution coloured modern Europe and eventually the rest of the world. In some respects it allowed the dialectic worked out by Karl Marx and Friedrich Engels to offer another new and very different vision for change. This time the ownership of the means of production was crucial to the argument, as was the assumption that capitalism would collapse through class conflict and that therefore, following these shifts, a new order would result. It was Lenin and the Bolsheviks who not only adopted this philosophy but also engineered the class conflict through violent revolution. Marx's philosophy, while partially resulting from a Judaeo-Christian model of the 'end-time', was self-consciously atheistic; his aphorism about religion being the opium of the people is admittedly often wrenched out of context. It follows a poetic, almost wistful sentence: 'Religion is the sigh of the oppressed creature, the heart of a heartless world, the soul of a soulless environment.' So Marx could see that religion had had a palliative effect but now he was clear that this soulless environment must go, and the illusions of religion must, alas, go with it. Lenin changed the preposition to crucial effect. For Lenin religion was an opium for the people. In Lenin's thought it takes on a more ominous feel and so it must go. So indeed it did go and the story of religion within the USSR is well known. Lenin and Khrushchev were arguably more cruel in persecution than was Joseph Dzhugashvili – that is, Josef Stalin. Nonetheless, one should not put Stalin's softening of the state's stance towards religion down to his brief period as an Orthodox seminarian in his native Georgia. Instead his softer stance in the 1940s was entirely linked to the political realities of waging war; he knew that attitudes in Russia linking nationalism and the Church were strong – his motives were utterly cynical.

It would be convenient and comforting to suggest that following the collapse of the Soviet Union religion has set the entire Russian nation alight. That would be a parody of the truth. It is the case, however, in Russia, Georgia and others of the former Soviet republics whose natural religion was Orthodox Christianity, that where religion has revived it does still feel like a natural religion. Those who attend the liturgy – of all ages – are at home in the ritual and have a sense of knowing how to worship which they apparently receive with their mother's milk. At its best, Christianity, where it now lives healthily in these republics, restores some heart to humanity. At its best, in the post Second World War period, the Christian Church was able, in other parts of the Soviet Empire, to act as the moral foundation for opposition to Russian imperialism and oppression. This was most obvious in Lithuania and Poland, and notably with Lech Walesa's Solidarity movement. Even in East Germany, as the Soviet Empire staggered to its collapse, the German Protestant Church, with support from the former West German Protestant churches, acted as a focus for resistance to Erich Honecker's hated regime.

This brief snapshot of two elements from within modern European history does give something of an answer to the question posed by John Lennon's song. Each day will bring its own concerns and anxieties but that is not the same as 'living for today'. To remove God from the equation will have a significant impact. This is not to imply naïvely that all religion is good religion, nor indeed that all Christianity is good Christianity. It is to argue, however, that when the Christian gospel is really lived, it can have a transforming effect upon society, upon individuals, and indeed upon the nature of our humanity and human civilization. As well as these non-theistic political models, there have been – and remain – other non-theistic visions too. 'Transcendental meditation', for example, has had its vogue from time to time. It was argued some years ago that if ten million people were to give themselves to a minimum of 15 minutes of such meditation each day then the world would be transformed. The fact is that if this is so then we are still awaiting the dénouement. This prediction is a shallow prophecy for two reasons. First of all, transcendental meditation is an entirely individual activity and discipline; societies change because both *individuals* and *groups* behave in a new and transformed way. Second, the fact of the matter is that the required practice set out above has never happened anyway, and it is hard to see how it could be achieved. This is not to suggest that such meditation is worthless, but rather to argue that it is not, and indeed never was, intended to be a salvific movement or religion. It has never claimed to relate to an objective external reference point or to God.

This brief analysis, however, does provoke the positive reflection that each of these visions, despite some admirable insights and often with admirable intentions, is lost without God. Part of the reason for this relates to the part which belief in God plays in helping human beings (and even societies) to become 'unselfed'. Selfishness is a universal aspect of our humanity and looking outwards from ourselves to a transcendent reference point can begin to undermine our instinctual selfish desires. Iris Murdoch, both in her novels and in her philosophy, while being clear that she was neither a Christian nor a theist, commended the practice of contemplation. She gives a vivid example at one point as to why contemplation is beneficial to human flourishing. Imagine yourself, she argues, sitting at your desk one morning, out of sorts and self-obsessed. Suddenly, and entirely as a gift, a kestrel comes into view hovering before the window. At once your gaze is set on the bird and your heart too is freed up. You look out from yourself. This transforms your mental attitudes, and removes purely selfish concerns. Such, she suggests, is the importance of contemplation.[7]

Iris Murdoch's insight here links with a long-cherished tradition within Christianity. In this ancient Christian tradition there is also an assumption that by offering ourselves to worship God and in giving time for contemplation again we can be unselfed and our lives can be transformed. So, in contrast to those philosophies and ideologies which reject God, allowing only some form of secular humanism, with the implicit danger of life turning in on oneself, both individuals and societies can turn their faces outwards towards God. In the twentieth century this tradition was most beautifully and effectively focused in Kenneth Kirk's book, *The Vision of God*. At one point Kirk writes:

> What is clear . . . is that Christianity came into a world tantalized with the belief that some men at least had seen God, and had found in that vision the sum of human happiness; a world aching with the hope that the same vision was attainable by all.[8]

As he began to explore that tradition within Christianity, he notes a little later:

> This means to say that Jesus, though he spoke little about 'seeing God' brought God more vividly before the spiritual eyes of his contemporaries than any other has ever done. He *gave* a vision of God where others could only *speak* of it.[9]

One of the remarkable things about Kirk's book is that he is able to show how this 'vision of God', that is, setting our eyes and our hearts on God in Jesus, can transform every part of our lives and of the life of our world, if others similarly are caught up into this vision. So for Kirk theology becomes not a series of specialisms focusing on belief, on worship, on contemplation and on the moral life. Instead it is a way of seeing the world, fashioned and patterned by that vision of God on which we have focused our hearts and minds. It is a pattern picked up by Kirk from the so-called Caroline Divines – Anglican priests and theologians writing in the seventeenth century. Here, then, we have that practical living out of the gospel which has been haunting us throughout, a practice which has not and cannot be matched in transcendental meditation, and a practice (even within the limits of its own philosophy) which has never fully been worked out within the Marxist framework. It is a pattern rooted in God, and lived out most perfectly in the life of Jesus. Jesus himself *lives out* what he *calls out* of all humanity, as we saw earlier in that saying in Matthew's Gospel:

> You, therefore, must be perfect, as your heavenly Father is perfect.[10]

This is the challenge to transform lives. In a sermon giving thanks for 50 years' witness of the Society of St Francis in 1971, Archbishop Michael Ramsey touched on this theme, as he suggested how the Franciscan life might offer a pattern for all. So, beginning from his text in Paul's second letter to the Corinthians, 'As having nothing, yet possessing everything', he goes on to say:

> 'As having nothing.' Go back to the Gospels. Jesus proclaimed the Kingdom of God, that is the reign, the sovereignty, the power of God. And those who accept the Kingdom, reign, sovereignty, power of God say goodbye to any claim to power in themselves, of themselves, for themselves. A rich man cannot get through a tiny needle's eye. Why? Because he is too big . . . But all this is not something special for friars or monks . . . it is the essential doctrine of the Kingdom of God, the 'all-ness' of God and the nothingness of the self in its own right or in its own terms . . . This is Christianity: *as having nothing.*[11]

So, using that same text (2 Cor. 6.10), the Archbishop shows how the friars in those 50 years had become foci of that same vision of God. At the end of the sermon, he reminded them too of St Francis' stigmata:

> So thank you, dear Franciscans, thank you for what you are, for what you do, for what you give the rest of us, in the truth of the

Gospel of Jesus and the apostles. God keep you near to the wounds of the Passion, near to the joy of Christ. And thanks be to the good God, who in his loving kindness would strip us of all things so that all things may be ours.

The sermon and the occasion still remain with me; I was there that day in Westminster Abbey. It was a powerful and moving message, and all the more so for one who was both a member of the Franciscan Third Order and would begin training for the priesthood in the following year.

Michael Ramsey's address to the Franciscans took him close to the theme which hauntingly recurs throughout his writings. He stood firmly within that stream of Anglican theologians whose most significant focus is on the incarnation. In Jesus Christ we can understand and relate to God most clearly and most fully. He returned to this theme again and again. So, for example, in 1962, in his introduction to the reprint of *Peake's Commentary on the Bible*, the Archbishop makes the point forcibly. Christianity is not a religion of a *book*, but instead of a *person*. So, however important the Bible is – and this was an introduction to a comprehensive commentary on the entire Bible – it is a source for understanding our faith. It is also the key source and authority for encountering the witness and person of Jesus Christ. The Bible, then, is chiefly important for helping us, both individually and in our corporate humanity, to encounter the person of Jesus Christ.

Some years later, Ramsey would encapsulate this truth in a memorable phrase or aphorism. He wrote: 'God is Christlike and in him is no un-Christlikeness at all.' The language here is vivid and makes clear that the nature of God for Christian people is enfleshed in the person of Jesus Christ. That is the sort of God in whom we believe and whom we worship. In addition to that, anything which is not Christlike is excluded from our understanding of God's nature. Ramsey goes on to clarify this and give it still greater vividness by rooting it in Jesus' death and vindication: The Christlikeness of God means that his [Jesus'] passion and resurrection are the key to the very meaning of God's own deity.' A little later he notes:

> So when God became incarnate as man his meaningfulness as God came into his own. The self-giving, the becoming-man, the suffering love were not additions to the divine experience or mere incidents in the divine history. In becoming man, God revealed the meaning of what it is to be God.[12]

These various reflections of Michael Ramsey, then, are about the way in which God enters our humanity; 'man' here, of course, refers to all humanity, both women and men. Ramsey helps us not only to appreciate the nature of the God whom we love and worship, but also to see the pattern of life which is called out of us. As we can see, the passion of Jesus and his total self-giving lie at the heart of this life. The vision of God commended by Kenneth Kirk is just such a vision and it calls out of us a similar life of self-giving. In the words of that text which Ramsey took from St Paul's second letter to the Corinthians: 'As having nothing yet possessing everything.' The passion, then, is not some form of mawkish, masochistic, eccentric part of Jesus' life and Christian faith. Instead it was the natural outcome within Jesus' life for the one who in living such a pattern of self-giving challenged the very essence of the culture of the time. Geoffrey Lampe puts it very powerfully:

> In Jesus' life and death, alike, God was acting towards sinners, breaking through their self-centred resistance and reconciling them to himself.

This then means that:

> The Cross is the ultimate sign of man's hatred, and in that very focal point of hatred the love of God accepts him despite the worst that he can do, in his most extreme sinfulness and bitter enmity.[13]

This is a pattern which is clear from the life of Jesus, not only as set out in the four Gospels, but also as in other scripted material within the New Testament. So in his letter to the Philippians, St Paul writes:

> Have this in mind among yourselves, which is yours in Christ Jesus, who, though he was in the form of God, did not count equality with God a thing to be grasped, but emptied himself, taking the form of a servant, being born in the likeness of men. And being found in human form he humbled himself and became obedient unto death, even death on a cross.[14]

The approach to God in Jesus set out here was later worked out in still more detail by Bishop John V. Taylor. His reflection on the 'Christ-like God' begins from the ways in which we acquire our own idea of God and then relates them both to the revelation unfolded in the Judaeo-Christian scriptures and in other traditions. Using the same

'Christlikeness' image of Michael Ramsey, Taylor also uses an image beloved of the novelist and theologian Charles Williams and the theologian Austin Farrer. The image is that of coinherence. In Jesus, we see God and humanity coinhere. In other words, our humanity and God's divinity permeate each other – it is a matter of divine–human exchange. In Jesus this happens perfectly, but in Jesus too we see this possibility being opened up for all humanity. It has, of course, its challenges for us. We often value our self-sufficiency. So Williams writes at one point:

> It is regarded as Christian to live 'for' others [but] it is not so often regarded as Christian doctrine that we live 'from' others – except certainly in rare experiences. There has been, everywhere, a doctrine of unselfishness, but that the self everywhere lives only within others has been less familiar.[15]

This passage encapsulates Williams' doctrine of coinherence and it leads also into a broader tradition strongly represented within Orthodox theology of *theiosis* or *divinization*. These rather technical words simply imply the possibility of God entering our humanity, assuming that from within our own humanity we are prepared to open ourselves to God's grace. We can allow God to fill us. This image becomes more vivid still as we reflect upon the grace we receive in baptism and confirmation, and in ordination. More widely and regularly still is that grace made available to us in the Eucharist and in the communion we then share with God. In all this, the self-giving nature of God in Jesus Christ is made plain, but so is the challenge to us to give of ourselves. Picking up the image of the forgiving father, in the parable that we know better as the 'prodigal son', John Taylor reflects:

> Each one of these figures of God [here the forgiving father], if that is what we take them to be, is at the receiving end of some wrong yet is never diminished or defeated. That is the Christlike God, and we should correct our conventional images accordingly for it is he alone whom we should adore and seek to resemble in the terms of this world's relationships.[16]

These reflections have brought us a long way from the values of the French Revolution and from the distortions of Marx's original vision, in that of Marxist-Leninism, in the vision of the Russian Revolution and all that followed from that. But how far have we come from John Lennon's imaginings? It is, perhaps, that final word from John Taylor that does indicate the distance that we have moved along the road. He reflects: 'That is the Christlike God, and we should correct our conventional images accordingly for it is he alone whom we should adore and seek to resemble in the terms of this world's relationships.' Lennon's instincts feel positive, but somehow the jump to the brotherhood of man, or of humanity, is made too easily. It is too rooted in *us*, and we all know the fallibility of our human nature. The journey that we have taken into the vision of God has taken us out of ourselves. It has also taken us into the heart of our God who in Jesus Christ is also the ultimate ex-ample of self-giving. In Jesus selfhood is offered up, allowing God's grace to fill him entirely. It is following that model that will allow us to pattern our relationships in this world so that they resemble those of that same Christlike God. In a popular piece by an unknown author, now widely available, this is well summed up as it reflects upon Jesus Christ:

> Nineteen wide centuries have come and gone, and today he is the centrepiece of the human race and the leader of all human progress. All the armies that ever marched, all the navies that were ever built, all the parliaments that ever sat, and all the kings that ever reigned, put together, have not affected the life of humanity upon this earth as powerfully as this one solitary life.

Some of this would be reformed in the multi-cultural world in which we are now set. But certainly the teaching and spirit of Jesus Christ remains transformative and lives at the very heart of the Christlike God, defining the Christian message and the Christian life. It is this Lord's song which we are called to sing in what often feels to be a strange land. It is a song which is about more than solely 'living for today'. Belief in God does effectively make all the difference. It is a belief which is shared with others. It is a pattern which throughout two millennia has helped define the Church. Imagine what that Church might be called to be . . .

4

The way old friends do
The Church

———◆•◆•◆———

Times of joy and times of sorrow
We will always see it through
Oh I don't care what comes tomorrow
We can face it together
The way old friends do.[1]

Abba took the 1970s and early 1980s by storm. They even convinced the cynics that the Eurovision Song Contest, that old lady of television, could sometimes get things right, since it was their victory there with 'Waterloo' that set them on the way to stardom. Some of their songs have become classics a quarter of a century later and their words easily spring to the lips even of those who were babes in arms at that time. The song that heads this chapter, however, has achieved something still more extraordinary; along with that other Abba hit, 'Happy New Year', it has become part of the eccentric repertoire of music, dance and miscellaneous celebration which come together to form that rich diet which makes up New Year's Eve. So, Abba songs are often used alongside 'Auld lang syne' and other old faithfuls as part of the wider treasury from which New Year's celebrations are made.

Celebration of what they call 'Old Year's Night', in Scotland and northern England, is a remarkable and exotic experience and it differs in character from place to place across the world. For example, in Germany it is almost de rigueur for families to watch a 25-minute comedy film, made by the veteran English comedian Freddie Frinton, perhaps two generations ago. The film's title is *Dinner for One*. It features dinner on New Year's Eve in the house of an aged English gentlewoman; it is served by her butler. The table set for six has only the hostess there – all the rest have died! It is very funny, but it is difficult to see why *Germans* should universally watch it. Often they watch it in English, with no sub-titles, and so the butler's frequently repeated comic mantra: 'Same procedure as last year, madam?' would appear to be lost without translation. Furthermore the film is rooted in the past glories of the English aristocracy, which is fairly well removed from the contemporary pattern of life in middle-class Germany. Yet whole families come together to watch the film, often with large numbers of friends.

In the north of England and in Scotland, the ritual of the 'first foot' still survives. The myth is that the family will receive a year of good luck if their first visitor is a tall dark male, carrying a piece of coal in one hand and a glass of some warming liquor in the other. These two symbols, received after midnight, represent first warmth for the family and then sustenance for the body, for the coming year, and the key factor is that they come from outside. It is a sign that the human community survives only if we work together. Perhaps the most extraordinary New Year celebrations in the world are those which happen in Scotland. The dancing of reels, the singing of Scottish folk songs, the dressing up in kilt and Scottish costume are now also mingled with icons of the present age, including Abba's 'Happy New Year' and 'The way old friends do', and indeed, much other music of the day. In Edinburgh this has now expanded into 'The Greatest Hogmanay on Earth'. So great has been the response that ticketing is now restricted and barriers are put up along the streets to avoid people being injured through the pressure of the crowds.

Although, then, New Year festivities are many and various and differ significantly across the world, there is one thing that is held in common. This common assumption is that this is a moment for celebrating human community and solidarity; this is a time for people to come together. It was seen still more vividly at the time of the passing of the new millennium. On that occasion there was a live television link across the world. People in Sydney, Vancouver, Cape Town, London and Prague could celebrate in unison – in virtual, if not in immediate terms. In all these cases, then, community is central. The Germans use Freddie Frinton as a focus for gathering friends and extended family. In the north of England, the 'first foot' brings comfort and reassurance that we are prepared to care for each other. Then a real Scottish Hogmanay brings people together as at no other time in the year. This reflection is in itself vital. For we live in a culture which has become increasingly individualistic. People are less inclined to join organizations: political parties, trade unions, paramilitary organizations and churches have all been affected. Alongside this it is also often difficult to gather people together for celebrations and jamborees. But the New Year experience runs counter to this. It reminds us that deep down there remains a human instinct for solidarity. 'Auld lang syne' captures it perfectly in the extraordinary dialect tones of Robert Burns:

> Should auld acquaintance be forgot
> And never brought to mind,
> Should auld acquaintance be forgot
> For the sake of auld lang syne.

Not only do we sing it, but we take the hands of others to form an imaginary circle around the globe. 'Finding comfort together', as Abba put it, 'the way old friends do.'

This is equally true of the Church of God, and therefore why it is important to gather Christian people together from time to time in large numbers. Greenbelt and Spring Harvest are two good examples of how this happens regularly. Some years ago the diocese of Portsmouth hosted a great gathering which focused deliberately on 'the vocation of the Church'. It brought together, within the 1,500 people who came, some 500 people below the age of 30. It aimed to offer all who came an appropriate self-confidence, helping them to realize that they were part of a much larger community than they ever imagined. A number of people, including my own older son, began to think of offering themselves for the ordained ministry as a result of that weekend. It was a good experience of solidarity with other Christian people.

Despite the rampant – and sometimes defiant – individualism of our contemporary world, there is underneath it all an unshakeable instinct which tells of our solidarity – not only in families, villages, cities and nations, but across the world. Those terrifying pictures and reports from Michael Buerk and Mike Wooldridge in Ethiopia, which we encountered earlier on, touched the consciences of people in every part of the globe. If one part of humanity suffers then we all suffer. Shylock's famous words touch the same nerve:

> Hath not a Jew eyes? Hath not a Jew hands, organs, dimensions, senses, affections, passions . . . If you prick us, do we not bleed? If you tickle us, do we not laugh? If you poison us, do we not die?[2]

Part of what Shylock was saying there, of course, was an attempt to relate the two separate sub-cultures and indeed two distinct religions – Christianity and Judaism – to each other. Shylock began there, then, with the same raw material encountered on Old Year's Night and New Year's Day, the raw material of our common humanity. Many years ago

I was talking to someone of his amazing success in business; he was a high achiever, but he had come from a family of very modest means. His father had been a coal miner in County Durham and had retired early through lung disease. Despite considerable poverty and serious illness, mother and father had helped their young son to succeed. They had supported him at school, even paying fees at one point, for it was a direct-grant grammar school which did not operate purely within the state system. I reflected fairly wistfully to him on one occasion: 'You must be enormously grateful to your parents for all their support which helped you to do so well.' 'Nonsense,' he replied, 'it was not my parents who achieved this, I did it *myself.*' Undoubtedly it was his determination that eventually saw him through, but it was a myopic reflection on his part that somehow discounted the part that others played in the process.

None of this, however, ignores the importance of the individual. Indeed, without motivation and determination high achievers would never reach their goals. Nevertheless, we very rarely achieve it entirely on our own. Recently the Shakespearean actor and star of television's *Star Trek: The Next Generation*, Patrick Stewart, was made Chancellor of the University of Huddersfield. A local lad from nearby Mirfield, Stewart was much moved by his appointment. One of his first responses was to nominate his former headmaster for an honorary degree at the same university. 'Without his support, inspiration and encouragement,' Stewart said, 'I would never even have become a professional actor.' Similarly, at the end of my own school career I lost all confidence in my ability in science and notably in physics. Never again would I volunteer to study science. Yet, as I prepared for my finals in my first degree I remember deliberately opting to focus particularly on the physics elements within a broader 'natural science' course. What an amazing turnaround. Things went happily, but only because an inspired teacher and a stimulating and cooperative set of fellow students were there with me to encourage me on my way.

All this may seem fairly obvious stuff, but it is not so clear or obvious in a competitive world where much store is placed on individual enterprise and achievement. Nonetheless, this holding together of our part in a wider humanity alongside our own individual personhood stands at the heart of the Christian gospel. We live and die both as individuals and as part of the wider human community. It is set out classically and with great energy by St Paul in the New Testament. We have already encountered Paul's realism about our individual sense of both aspiration and failure:

I do not understand my own actions. For I do not do what I want, but I do the very thing I hate . . . I can will what is right but I cannot do it.[3]

Some feel that Paul is too hard here both on himself and on our individual humanity across the board. Certainly, his declaration that 'I know that nothing good dwells within me' may feel unduly harsh. But his sense of both aspiration and fallibility ring true to all of us. We hold out great hopes and desire to do good things, not just for ourselves but for others too. Yet so often we fall short of these hopes, and frequently this may cause distress to others as well as for ourselves.

Elsewhere, however, Paul makes it abundantly clear that we did not simply need to be saved *individually* from *ourselves*, but that we need also to be saved as part of all humanity, *in solidarity with others*. In other words it is our humanity as much as our individuality that needs to be redeemed. The first remarkable eight chapters of his letter to the Romans work this out on the broadest of possible canvases. His own experience of having been liberated from pure selfishness, being 'unselfed', as we described it in the previous chapter, leads him to understand how God, in Jesus Christ, has liberated all humanity. In solidarity with all, as individuals we have been liberated, saved, redeemed, set free. Different words speak more vividly to different ages and different cultures. Nonetheless the root experience is the same. Earlier on in the letter to the Romans, this is set out with great clarity. Paul compares the old Israel in Adam to the new Israel in Christ. Abraham, who is the father of many nations, becomes the 'type' whom we have been destined to follow in Christ. Abraham is a pattern of true faith. Israel is seen in solidarity with Abraham.[4] We are called to emulate Abraham by being people of faith. The death and resurrection of Jesus Christ is then the one event which transforms all humanity. This is the ground of our faith. The relationship of *all humanity* to God has been set right in Jesus. Comparing Jesus to Adam (who is the type for our fallen humanity), Paul writes:

For if the many died through the one man's trespass, much more surely have the grace of God and the free gift in the grace of one man, Jesus Christ, abounded for the many . . . Therefore just as one man's trespass led to condemnation for all, so one man's act of righteousness leads to justification and life for all.[5]

This, then, really does mean that we can face it together, 'the way old friends do'. It was presumably this sort of realization that led the trade unionists in Poland in the 1970s and 1980s to call their organization

45

Solidarity. Lech Walesa and those who followed him had been nurtured in a Catholic view of the Christian faith that requires humanity to be seen as a whole. Human beings can only thrive in community and in solidarity with each other. Nevertheless, our own individual culpability and the culpability of the whole human race can and must be kept together. They cannot be separated, for the two are interdependent. Paul's great canvas in those first eight chapters of his letter to the Romans, then, describes theologically what God has done for humanity in Jesus. God achieves human liberation or redemption in the pattern of life, in the manner of death, and through the vindication of both that life and that death, in the resurrection of Jesus Christ. It is that same pattern of life alluded to right at the beginning of this book, in the introduction.

In that introduction we also indicated that the pattern of life in God, lived out in Jesus and followed later within the apostolic communities, is one which is repeated and developed in the early Church and more generally in the life of the great variety of Christian communities which have existed down the centuries. Indeed the Church helps us to see that our liberation or redemption occurs not only as individuals but also within the context of humanity as a whole. Community and solidarity then are integral to the Christian life. Paul is once again at pains to make this clear without describing in any institutional way what we would now call the Church. He makes it very clear that the responsibility for both living and proclaiming this redemption (in word and deed) now rests with us. All this is described in an inspired passage in his second letter to the Corinthians. He writes:

> From now on, therefore, we regard no one from a human point of view; even though we once knew Christ from a human point of view, we know him no longer in that way. So if anyone is in Christ, there is a new creation: everything old has passed away; see, everything has become new. All this is from God, who reconciled us to himself through Christ, and has given us the ministry of reconciliation; that is, in Christ God was reconciling the world to himself, not counting their trespasses against them, and entrusting the message of reconciliation to us. So we are ambassadors for Christ, since God is making his appeal through us . . .[6]

Elsewhere, Paul puts it even more directly:

> Think of us in this way, as servants of Christ and stewards of God's mysteries.[7]

Paul is clear, then, that we have a definite commission, and certainly this has been the baton which the Church took up from Jesus and the apostles, so it believed, and which it has passed on relay by relay from generation to generation. But what is it that we are to pass on and what is it that we are to commend to all humanity? On one level we could simply say that it is what has just been set out above. In Jesus Christ, God set humanity free. That is too terse and limited, however, on its own. God's Church is also to live out that pattern seen quintessentially in Jesus. What does that pattern include? The answer is, of course, an enormously rich treasury. It is captured classically in the New Testament. Even there the richness is such that it is described in a variety of complementary ways. The life and ministry of Jesus is pictured vividly but differently in the four Gospels. The Lord's song is sung there by Jesus himself and it certainly feels as if he too is singing God's song in a strange land. Stevie Smith captures this perfectly in her poem, 'The Airy Christ':

As he knows the words he sings, that he sings so happily
Must be changed to working laws, yet sings he ceaselessly.

Those who truly hear the voice, the words, the happy song,
Never shall need working laws to keep from doing wrong.

Deaf men will pretend sometimes they hear the song, the words,
And make excuse to sin extremely; this will be absurd.

Heed it not. Whatever foolish men may do the song is cried
For those who hear, and the sweet singer does not care that he was
    crucified

For he does not wish that men should love him more than anything
Because he died; he only wishes they would hear him sing.[8]

Paul responds to that life and death in his letters, as do all the other New Testament authors. In the Apocalypse, the Revelation to John, that impact is described differently again. What, then, precisely are the key elements that we encounter in the impact of Jesus?

Perhaps the one element which is most striking is that of reconciliation. Reconciliation brings people together. But it may nevertheless be a prophetic reconciliation; we see that clearly on the one occasion when we encounter Jesus behaving violently, as he cleanses the Temple. Nonetheless, elsewhere violence is avoided completely and generally reconciliation is effected through acceptance. The description of Jesus in his trial is of someone who has utterly accepted that he must live a life patterned by God's grace. W. H. Vanstone, in his book *The Stature of Waiting*, puts this very powerfully. He asks why Judas ever needed to betray Jesus. After all, as Jesus himself says at one point, all he did he did openly. Vanstone points out that the word translated as 'betray' also means to 'hand over'. Judas, then, hands Jesus over and thereafter Jesus allows himself to be 'done to' rather than to do. Vanstone gives vivid examples of how this has been lived out too in individual human lives. He talks of a bishop who in the last few months of his life became virtually incapable of any action. He lay supine on the bed. Nevertheless this holy man showed his godliness no less in his passivity than he had in his earlier active life.[9]

Passivity and acceptance are not the totality of what is required in the process of reconciliation but they are key elements. In the parable of the forgiving father or prodigal son, in St Luke's Gospel, we see set out there an integrated but complex pattern of reconciliation. Although the older son is not fully reconciled, as far as we can see, still the father has established a pattern of behaviour which allows reconciliation to occur, if others will only allow God's grace to work in them and receive that reconciliation. Again and again within the Gospels, Jesus faces hostility, and his response is not to be drawn, but instead to use the occasion either for teaching or to bring people together.

> Those who truly hear the voice, the words, the happy song,
> Never shall need working laws to keep from doing wrong.

Often his healing miracles themselves seem to imply a deeper reconciliation with God. Then, in yet another different context, the encounter with the Samaritan woman at Jacob's Well shows Jesus responding to a woman who has lived a disordered life becoming reconciled to the pattern of God's grace.[10] Paul, as we have seen, is quite clear that the message we have been given is one of reconciliation.

> All this is from God, who through Christ reconciled us to himself and gave us the ministry of reconciliation; that is, in Christ God was reconciling the world to himself, not counting their trespasses against them, and entrusting to us the message of reconciliation.[11]

In Chapter 2, we encountered two clear examples of the Church, or at least a community within the Church, helping to bring reconciliation between peoples. The Community of Sant'Egidio was the broker for peace in both Mozambique and Uganda. Reconciliation of this sort, Christians believe, is part of God's desire for humanity. In these circumstances the Church stands for *humanity before God* and for *God before humanity*. It manifests, then, a priestly role as it seeks to bring reconciliation between people. There are admittedly far too many examples of the Church or churches bringing discord rather than reconciliation between peoples. The period of the European Reformation is probably that era in which the Church's record in this report is most sullied. Even since then, however, different churches have failed to be reconciled to each other to such a degree that this has been the cause of internecine conflict. In Ireland, for example, it is only fairly recently that the churches have taken the initiative in the process of reconciliation between communities. There is an element here of 'Physician, heal thyself.' Until churches learn how to be reconciled to each other ecumenically they will not offer a happy model to the wider community. In recent years the Anglican Communion has not even been very effective in handling the process of reconciliation internally.

Despite these rather depressing examples, however, there is no doubt that a key part of the Church's vocation is to point to reconciliation and that this reconciliation is itself rooted in God. In bringing reconciliation it is acting out a priestly role on behalf of God and on behalf of all humanity. This is part of the key to understanding the ministerial priesthood within God's Church. It is first and foremost, then, the Church that is priestly. Moreover, priesthood by no means exhausts that pattern of Christlike life which God's Church is called to live and commend to others. What else ought the Church to be mirroring in Christ?

Another key element within the pattern of life which Jesus both lived and died for, is that of service. This is a translation of the New Testament word *diakonia*. Since this is the key root word for ministry in the New Testament, we could have begun here in our reflection on the vocation of God's Church and on what comprises that vocation. We avoided beginning here, however, since the word *diakonia*, and those words associated with it, present us with a background of considerable complexity within the New Testament itself. The word *diakonia* and many of its associated or derived words are those which we would now translate with the general term 'ministry'. Nonetheless the word *diakonos*, as well as being translated sometimes simply as 'minister' or even 'servant', is also the technical term for a specific ministry in the New Testament. It is the word which we generally translate as 'deacon'.

What then might it mean to describe part of that pattern of the Church's life, modelled on Jesus Christ, as diaconal? Most generally of all it could simply refer to the Church as a 'ministering Church'. That, however, does not get us much further and indeed is why this book is not about ministry in a general sense, but instead seeks to focus on 'representative' public ministry. Many years ago, Helen Oppenheimer described ministry as a 'greedy' concept.[12] By this she means that ministry can describe that which all Christian people have been called to do, but also specific ministries offered by individual ministers. If we accept that ministry can be used in a general sense then we need to differentiate a more specific use when it is applied to deacons. In this case it has often been seen to refer to *humble service*, rather like the references in the Acts of the Apostles to deacons serving at tables.[13] More recently a new and broader interpretation has been put forward which suggests a role as a messenger.[14] We shall look at this debate in a later chapter, when we look specifically at the ministry of deacons. At this stage, however, the key point to register is that Jesus' ministry undoubtedly was one of service, and most obviously in the context of his life (and death) of utter self-giving.

> For he does not wish that men should love him more than anything
> Because he died; he only wishes they would hear him sing.

The Church, then, is called to be a servant Church and this will manifest itself in any number of different ways. Within the Lutheran tradition, *diakonia* has most generally been interpreted as social responsibility and aid for the developing world. One vivid example will suffice here. When in 1990, the Archbishop of Canterbury at that time, Dr Robert Runcie, visited Ethiopia, he was able through the unblocking of diplomatic channels to ensure that promised aid would now get to the war and famine-torn areas of that then beleaguered country. A substantial amount of this aid was being supplied by the *diakonia* departments of the Lutheran churches in Scandinavia and in Germany. This aspect of *diakonia* is a powerful way of serving the world in the name of Jesus Christ. It stands alongside similar work in many other churches. So, the Anglican Church in Australia offers support to poor communities through day-centres and residential care homes organized through its 'Anglicare' network. The Church of England, through the commitment of countless individual parishes, offers social support in a host of different ways and through a great variety of different local projects. This is a key part of the Church's diaconal vocation and engages thousands of lay people as well as clergy across the world.

Since the 1960s there has been an increasing emphasis on the concept of the 'servant Church'. It is but one model among many, including the

Church as sacrament, herald of the Kingdom, communion and insti-tution.[15] Even so, it is a model of the Church which takes us to the heart of the life, ministry, passion, death and resurrection of Jesus himself. For that reason there has been a continuing tradition, from earliest times, of individuals being ordained as *deacons* to represent, as ministers, the dia-conal ministry of Christ. Later we shall look at the ministry of deacons in more detail, but it is essential to see that the individual representative ministry of both priests and deacons issues first and foremost from the nature of the Church. Essentially it is the Church which is called to be both *diaconal* and *priestly*. That is where vocation is located. Individual ministers focus that nature and that quality or charism within the Church, in a sacramental way. So vocation and ministry spring from the nature of God which in turn patterns the life of the Church. From this issue the specific ministerial patterns of priesthood, diaconate and episcopate which we have inherited from the early Church.[16] Here we might delay for a moment, then, on bishops. Episcopal ministry too derives from our understanding of God. At the heart of our belief about the nature of God is the essential unity within the Godhead. Trinitarian-ism – that is, an understanding of God as Father, Son and Holy Spirit – has never allowed Christian belief in 'God as one' to be impaired. Christianity is a monotheistic religion. That key belief is repeated every time we say or sing the Nicene Creed: 'We believe in *One* God.' That same unity is echoed in the nature of the Church. Further on in the Creed we affirm: 'We believe in *One* Holy, Catholic and Apostolic Church.' That unity within the Church is, then, once again mirrored by the bishop. The bishop is the 'focus of unity'; the bishop defines the Church in a particular place by being the person to whom all members and parishes of the local Church turn for jurisdiction and pastoral care. The same pattern, beginning with God, modelled by the Church, and then focused sacramentally in an individual minister, follows.

There are, of course, other recognized vocations and ministries to which we shall return, but at this point it may be helpful to locate them, once again, in a theology of God's Church. The two most widespread, but very different, ministries upon which we shall concentrate are the *religious life* and the office of *reader*. The religious life is itself remarkably diverse and we shall look at different communities and 'rules' later on. From where, however, did the religious life spring? It would be wrong to see monasticism, and the religious life more generally, as part of a Christian monopoly. Both solitary and community vocations are to be found in other religious traditions. So the Essenes, who lived in the desert alongside the Dead Sea, and from whom most people assume the

Dead Sea Scrolls emerged, were a form of Jewish religious community. That in itself is interesting, since it was from origins within the desert that the Christian monastic tradition sprang. Both St Jerome, in the late fourth century, in the Syrian desert, and St Anthony, a little earlier on in the Egyptian desert, pioneered a form of withdrawal from the world. In those early days the so-called 'Desert Fathers' tended to live either entirely alone as hermits, or as 'semi-hermits' grouped around a common church. It was not until the time of Benedict, in the early sixth century, that monasticism began to emerge in a community form, as we might now understand it.

The religious life is often seen as a rebellion against the values of the world. Certainly it is true that in many communities the religious vows commit sisters, monks, friars and others to an austere life, often including a renunciation of personal possessions. Nonetheless, it may still be more appropriate to see the religious life as one more way of individuals, or individuals within community, focusing on particular aspects of the Christian life and perhaps doing so vicariously – that is, on behalf of the rest of us. This avoids the trap of understanding the Christian life as being lived within a double standard: that is, an easier worldly life for most of us and a tougher 'first-class' Christian life for a self-elected élite. The life of contemplative prayer, then, can be valued for what it is. It is a life which is only possible for some but it is a crucial witness which helps nourish us all. It is not a 'waste of a life' as some all too easily suggest. The same thing may be said of 'active' religious orders which are either missionary – that is, mainly concerned with running parish missions – or offer a life of care for others within community. In a different way, then, from priests, deacons and bishops, those called to the religious life focus for us key elements within the broader Christian life. We may indeed have the capacity to offer ourselves within this tradition. There are even possibilities to offer our lives in this way for those of us who are married and have families.[17]

Some of the most inspiring figures within Christian history have been *religious* (that is, called to the religious life), from great scholars to reformers, from martyrs to prophets. Some of these have been ordained but by no means all of them. St Anselm, the most outstanding scholar-Archbishop of Canterbury, was a Benedictine monk; St Thomas Aquinas, the remarkable systematic theologian, was a Dominican monk; Gregor Mendel, the pioneer of genetics, was a monk; St Teresa of Avila was a pioneering mystic. In the last century, Trevor Huddleston, the prophetic and tireless worker for racial justice, was a monk; Brother Roger founded the Taizé Community, which has been such an outstanding inspiration to young people. Mother Teresa gave her life to the poor of Calcutta. Those called to the religious life, then, focus some aspects of the gospel in a particular way. If it is not pressing the image too far, they too sing the Lord's song, but the echoes of it come to us as Gregorian chant and not in the freer hymnody and song which may fill our own days!

Then, in contrast to the religious life, and looking around the Church of our day, there is within the Church of England one other very substantial group of people to whom we shall again return later. This group of *readers* trace their origins back to the nineteenth century and were originally know as lay readers. This earlier name reminds us that readers exercise a ministry which is authorized within a national framework but they are deliberately not ordained; indeed, most readers cherish their lay status fondly. Readers are not without a longer pedigree. In the mediaeval Church there were so-called catechists and other forms of authorized teachers. Readers emerged as a group in the Church of England at a time when there was an increasing need for others, alongside ordained ministers, to read the offices of Morning and Evening Prayer. As time passed this ministry developed into a preaching and teaching ministry. Some readers now have a clear pastoral remit, but the heart of the reader's ministry is an educational and proclamatory role. Once again, alongside this clear function of assisting in services and study groups, readers also help to focus part of the wider teaching responsibility within God's Church. So the same principle applies as before. It is the whole Church which has the responsibility for living the gospel in its preaching and teaching role. Readers, however, in a representative public way, as lay people, help focus this important part of the Church's role in 'singing for all the Lord's song'.

In this chapter, then, we have been describing and celebrating the Church of God and its part in singing the Lord's song. We began on New Year's Eve, with Abba reminding us how we find 'comfort together, the way old friends do'. We discovered the importance of our part within one mutually supportive humanity. Our individual lives, and the healthiness of those lives, will not survive if we allow ourselves to become isolated and alone. The Church itself is a product of that wider humanity, called out by God to live the life we see in Jesus Christ. The Church under God represents our solidarity together with all humanity but which is then further powered by God's grace. Both our humanity and that grace are given by God; they are not the proud product of our own efforts. For God takes us out of ourselves and does that for the whole Church too. That gives the Church some very significant responsibilities within wider society. Some years ago, John Habgood, then Archbishop of York, crystallized those responsibilities and set them particularly within the context of an established Church. The Church's key responsibilities within society are, he argued, twofold. First of all,

> To hold in trust for the whole church, and for all religious bodies, the nation's religious commitment, i.e., its recognition of the place and importance of religion and religious freedom.

It does this not jealously or pompously but with some humility, knowing the greatness of the treasure which it inherits. This acknowledgement then takes us to Habgood's second principle. The Church, he argues, is called or has a vocation:

> To discover a language in which society may discuss itself in transcendental terms, and agree on common values to inform its public ethics and policies.[18]

These are profound responsibilities, describing a key vocation for the Church in our own society and in the wider world. The Church will not always get its responsibilities right and will often find itself under criticism both from outside and from inside for its apparent incapability of living out fully the vocation which it has inherited. At times the Church is seen to interfere too much. On other occasions it is seen to be too timid. Sometimes the Church is exhorted to be more aggressive in denouncing apparent attacks upon the gospel from contemporary popular culture. There are numerous examples of this, some more vivid than others. A generation ago, in response to such a criticism, many in the Church, bishops included, tried to get Monty Python's *Life of Brian* banned. At the very least Christians should boycott it, they said. I went along to see it, wearing my clerical collar, and the young lady at the pay kiosk looked at me askance. Some years later a similar commotion broke out in response to Martin Scorsese's film version of *The Last Temptation of Christ*. Responding to all the fuss, Bernard Levin, a very sympathetic Jewish agnostic, reflected, beginning with *Othello*:

> 'For Christian shame put by this barbarous brawl.' Yes, do, dear Christians all, and let me show you why you should. Jesus was put to death under Pontius ('Quod scripsi, scripsi' [what I have written, I have written]) Pilate, in the most painful and humiliating form of death then known. Dwell on it a for moment, please; I have a reason for asking. Christ was nailed to the cross through

his hands and feet, after being mocked, scourged and crowned with thorns. He was stabbed in the side by a spear, and when, dying, he asked for water, he was given vinegar. Through this prolonged ordeal, he was jeered by the spectators.

Meanwhile, how about Pilate? He was eventually recalled to Rome, though not in disgrace, despite the fact he couldn't stop the Jews talking (who could?). No one knows how he died, or when . . . And yet I must ask: which of them ended up with more egg on his face – Christ or Pilate? Assuredly Pilate, and not only because many millions now revere Christ and few him. I trust you see what I am getting at; in case not, I shall put it in the most demotic terms. For a man who has been crucified, having a film made about him is a doddle.[19]

These are salutary words for a Church which all too easily becomes defensive in singing its Lord's song, for remember:

Heed it not. Whatever foolish men may do the song is cried
For those who hear, and the sweet singer does not care that he was crucified.

That salutary reflection from Levin speaks to those who already are giving themselves, or those who think they might offer themselves, as ministers in God's Church. For the key thing to remember is to keep singing the Lord's song with the Church, 'finding comfort together the way old friends do'. We sing that song chorally and not just as a solo performance. Old Year's Night and New Year's Day are not bad places upon which to reflect, with all their resonances of joy and sorrow. It is to such joys and sorrows that individuals are called to minister within the broader vocation of God's Church. They may be called as deacons, as monks, as sisters or readers, as friars or priests. Part of the Christian journey is to discern whether each of us is called to one of those specific ministries within the vocation of God's Church.

5

Bridge over troubled water

Priesthood

———•◆•———

Simon and Garfunkel produced some of the most evocative music of the 1960s. They somehow captured both the mood of excitement and celebration, and also the feelings of angst and uncertainty. The 1960s, perhaps like the 1920s, were a decade of bubbling activity and nervous tension. The picture of Simon and Garfunkel on New York's Queens-boro or 59th Street Bridge reminds us of two of their greatest hits. One was '59th Street Bridge song', which encouraged us to feel 'groovy'. The other was 'Bridge over troubled water' – the fretted iron of the slightly rusting New York bridge once again set the scene.

'Bridge over troubled water' was arguably the greatest of all the hit songs recorded by Simon and Garfunkel. Alongside its excellent lyrics and haunting music, it somehow caught the mood of the time. It is not difficult to see why it might do this at any time, for it touches upon a familiar human mood. When one is feeling downcast or simply feeling low, one reaches out for others. Who will show empathy at this moment? Who will understand how I feel? Who will offer a helping hand? The lyrics respond to this mood directly. Indeed, the image of the bridge has been a key concept over the centuries. Humanity's ability to throw a bridge over a seemingly impassable divide has itself a sense of romance to it. It is true literally as well as metaphorically. The Golden Gate Bridge spanning the panoramic entrance to San Francisco Harbour, the Forth Railway Bridge marching its way over that great Scottish firth or indeed the Queen Elizabeth II Bridge to the east of London bridging the Thames on lofty pylons and carrying the capital's orbital motorway – all are great icons of modern engineering. Even a tiny stone clapper-bridge on Dartmoor, or the stately shop-lined Pulteney Bridge in Bath speak of more than their simple utilitarian function. They bring things together which are separated or sometimes even alienated from each other.

Simon and Garfunkel's song, of course, goes much deeper than this in its resonances. It hints at a picture of friendship whereby those things which need to be carried by one for another will be looked after with appropriate support and care. It implies too that there will hopefully always be a way through: apparent contradiction may find resolution; serious estrangements and breakdowns in relationship may be reconciled; even some of our more bizarre and irrational projections may be received by another, held there, and then somehow disarmed and relieved of their destructive power. All these images come close to those reflections explored in our previous chapter. God, in Jesus Christ, reconciles humanity in every way. We are reconciled to God. We too are given the potential to be reconciled to each other. The Church is given part of the responsibility for this by acting as the key instrument in our world for that process of reconciliation. But at present this still all feels to be on the level of theory and ideas. Simon and Garfunkel's song gives substance and flesh to this on the human level.

It is this set of experiences catalogued above that fairly swiftly moves Christians to talk of priesthood. For the Church, as God's instrument of reconciliation, also needs to be given flesh and substance. The institution on its own cannot reconcile. The Church is, after all, people. It will be people, individually or in groups, who can help enflesh this experience of reconciliation. Just one tragic story will make this point. Some 25 years ago Jean was returning home by car after doing an errand for somebody nearby in her own town. She was driving slowly through the estate on which she lived when a tiny child ran out in front of her. She jammed on the brakes, but there was nothing she could do; the child died before her eyes. She was, understandably, heartbroken and traumatized by the tragedy. Staggering about in her own personal darkness, she knew that she must do something. Having found out the address of the child's parents, with great courage she went to visit them. Not surprisingly they too were shattered by the tragedy. Even so, and despite their grief, they welcomed Jean in and made it clear that she could not possibly be held to blame; the child had somehow escaped from a well-fenced garden – it was no one's *fault*. Not only did they make it clear that Jean was not culpable, they empathized with her in her own grief. Both parents were Christian believers and both explained how their faith, and their local church and clergy, gave them support and counsel as they worked to rebuild their lives. Jean was amazed and strengthened by the experience in a remarkable way. It challenged her to recover an active faith, and some ten years later she was herself ordained.

This one simple story, which could be paralleled by so many others, takes us towards the heart of a reconciling priesthood. The essence of priesthood is in *being there* with people, not only in times of tragedy but also in times of joy and, just as importantly, in the more mundane periods of people's lives. Reflecting upon the life of all Christian people, St Paul captures it powerfully in his letter to the Romans. He writes:

> Bless those who persecute you; bless and do not curse them. Rejoice with those who rejoice, weep with those who weep.[1]

Once again it is this experience of solidarity that is essential. This time it is a 'one-to-one' solidarity, and it stands central to the Church's reconciling work and to the reconciling work of the individual priest. For it assures people of the inexhaustible and ever-present love of God in spite of all that the world can throw at them. This also takes us deeper into our relationship with God. For often the experiences that the priest will encounter will include significant breakdowns in relationship, either among individuals themselves, or between individuals and God. We can often feel ourselves to be falling short of what we would wish to be doing. How does God respond to our failure to live by the light which is given to us? We have already encountered the foundations of an answer to this question in the previous chapter when we looked briefly at St Paul's panoramic view of God and humanity. Humanity has been redeemed in *solidarity*:

> Therefore just as one man's trespass led to condemnation for all, so one man's act of righteousness leads to justification and life for all.[2]

At this point, however, we encounter this specifically in the context of the individual. How do we explain this forgiveness which God has promised? How do we explain the fact that each of us has been 'set right' with God, if we have faith? The answer to this has been set out in any number of ways, throughout Christian history, in different theories of the *atonement*. This word says just what it means if we split it into three: at-one-ment. In other words, this doctrine offers us an image of how we are made to be at one – that is, set right – with God. Numerous different images and models have been used to explain this, and this is not the place to examine all or even some in detail.[3] Suffice to say that some of these theories offer too harsh a view of God. God sacrifices Jesus to pay for our sins; this does not offer an attractive or convincing picture of an ever-loving God. Some other alternative theories fail for the opposite reason. Jesus becomes simply the model of a good man and the objective reality of evil is not taken seriously. Did Jesus' life of utter self-giving really make any difference?

Let us take just one recent model to help us understand how individuals are set right by God in Jesus. Any model that we might use must take the above factors into account; it must also set them within our contemporary understanding of human nature. So, we shall look at a psychological theory that may help us in understanding something of what is going on here. The model is that of *projective identification*, pioneered by Melanie Klein. In this theory the client projects his or her anger on to the psychologist or therapist with all the force that can be mustered. The therapist is there to 'hold' the projection, and then through the process of analysis and counselling is able to hand the anger back in a neutralized or indeed harmless form to the person whence it came. This may help us to understand something of the activity of God in Jesus Christ. All humanity, and each of us individually, effectively projects our sin and alienation on to the person of Jesus. Jesus through the all-pervading presence of God within him accepts and forgives, and our feelings and actions return to us disarmed, so to speak, so that we are set right with God.[4] This time the model is used theologically and not psychologically. These reflections remind us why it is the priest who also has the responsibility to pronounce God's absolution of our sins. It is, of course, God who absolves, but the priest is the person upon whom the confession is placed, so to speak, but not in this case projected. The process of identifying and nailing specific sins and omissions brings a reality that would otherwise be missing. The ministry of absolution, the sacrament of penance or reconciliation as it is also called, is just part of the wider sacramental role of the priest; it catches up part of God's reconciling love.

This brief reflection on priesthood and atonement offers us one further theological anchorhold which also vividly shows us how those human relationships which lie at the centre of an individual priest's ministry are part of the divine relationship too. The priest does not stand between God and each of us, but instead acts as a midwife to that relationship. To repeat a phrase used earlier, priests stand before God with humanity upon their hearts and, at the same time, before humanity with God etched upon their hearts. This model of divine–human exchange is not something which is achieved cheaply or without cost. We touched on this earlier when we quoted W. H. Vanstone's phrase 'love's endeavour, love's expense'. Vanstone, by using a number of vivid images and stories, points to the costliness of the human–divine relationship for God. He tells of an operation which, as a student, a doctor observed within a London hospital:

It was the first time that this particular brain operation had been carried out in this country. It was performed by one of our leading surgeons upon a young man of great promise for whom, after an accident, there seemed to be no other remedy. It was an operation of the greatest delicacy, in which a small error would have had fatal consequences. In the outcome the operation was a triumph: but it involved seven hours of intense and uninterrupted concentration on the part of the surgeon. When it was over, a nurse had to take him by the hand, and lead him from the operating theatre like a blind man or a little child.

Vanstone notes:

This, one might say, is what self-giving is like: such is the likeness of God, wholly given, spent and drained in that sublime self-giving which is the ground and source and origin of the universe.[5]

This model once again locates human endeavour in relation to God's endeavour. It also helps us see how the Church's vocation of service to the world mirrors God's self-giving and roots the priestly life of the individual within this same locus. Just like that surgeon, the priest will often be drained too. Sometimes it will admittedly be at a far more trivial level. As a young curate I would spend many afternoons visiting individual parishioners. This could be demanding, tiring and frustrating. Often you might call on a parishioner newly moved in, whom you were welcoming to the parish; they might not see your visit quite like that – the last person they were hoping to see was a clergyman. Or there were the difficult people, those who wished you were the vicar and not just the curate, or those who simply always moaned and complained. Even at this comparatively trivial level, the life of the priest can be demanding. Oh for the person who gave as much to you as you could ever possibly give to him or her!

On a more serious level, I remember little Heather, just four months old and diagnosed with leukaemia. With the advances made in the past 20 years she would probably still be alive today. Then, however, it was not to be. I visited Heather in Oxford's Radcliffe Infirmary, week after week. The emotional strain on her parents was enormous, but I too felt dragged down by it. Little Heather died, after far too short a life, and on a wretched windy and bleak February day I laid her to rest on the equally bleak and windswept hillside of Headington Cemetery. It was an in-explicable catalogue of suffering. There was no explaining it away. Yet, by a remarkable, generous and loving irony, Heather's parents came to faith through the tragedy, and just over a year later I baptized Helen, who would have been a 'little sister' to Heather. Belief in God, in spite of all their suffering, made more sense to Helen's parents than the desperate emptiness of Edwin Muir's account in his poem 'A Child Dying' which we encountered earlier. There are many other examples of such turnarounds and generally they are still very demanding for all involved. So, one woman priest had retained her faith through the experience of losing a baby who had been born prematurely and anencephalically. Out of the trauma of this terrible suffering, her husband too eventually offered himself for ordination.

It is easy to romanticize the life of the priest in telling such stories. It is thus important to set it all within the context of God's love. The moral of W. H. Vanstone's book is that God's love is inexhaustible. God does not hold back from pouring out love. This is true even when that love seems to be emptying out into meaningless chasms, formed by humanity's mutual inhumanity, or indeed other chasms formed by the apparent inescapable selfishness or self-indulgence of one or a number of individuals. This is what Vanstone means by talking of 'love's endeavour and love's expense'. He is not arguing, of course, that human love is similarly inexhaustible. It is crucial to realize this when reflecting upon the life of the ordained minister. We are human and not divine and there will be moments when our own supplies of stamina – physical, psychological and spiritual – will be exhausted. Owen Chadwick clearly felt like this on that day after the bomb fell in Huddersfield. Only the grace of God would get him through.

We have spoken a lot, then, about reconciliation, but we have not avoided mentioning the costliness of such a process, both to God and indeed to the Church and the individual priest. Talk of both atonement and absolution reinforce this sense of costliness, and it is there in the lyrics of the song which has set our theme of priesthood: they capture feelings of loneliness and uncertainty, feelings too of being assailed by troubles with no one to put things right. Who will be our companion within the storms of life? The song promises that however things develop, someone will be there to take our burdens and carry them. They will act as a 'bridge over troubled water'.

There is also another element to this ministry of reconciliation which is there too in the Gospels and in the life of Jesus. There are occasions when times may need to become rough before true reconciliation can occur. When Jesus overturns the tables in the Temple, he is engaging in a single symbolic and *prophetic* act. Unless there is real change in the way in which humans respond to their God, there can be no real reconciliation. This is the message of this episode; it was almost a political act. This element of the prophetic is also part of the priestly vocation of the Church and of individual ministers ordained to the priesthood. This means, then, that on occasion the Church will be unavoidably caught up in politics. Politicians are often uneasy with this, and frequently the Church and clergy are told to keep out of politics. Admittedly, it is rarely helpful for either the Church or individual priests to be identified too easily with any one political party. Even here, however, when there is real injustice it may be necessary to support a particular group or party which is attempting to resist the tendency towards such evil. What do we mean here?

One outstanding example of such evil occurred during the 1930s when Adolf Hitler and the Nazi party managed to persuade a large body of Protestant churchmen and women to collude with them in forming a church which effectively would become a puppet of the state. This provoked the formulation of the Barmen Declaration; the subsequent formation of the 'Confessing Church', following this declaration, was a chosen and deliberate political act aimed at staking out a defiant Christian witness in opposition to Nazi oppression and totalitarianism. Alongside this, Bishop George Bell of Chichester worked with Dietrich Bonhoeffer and others in putting together an international and united front against Hitler's tyranny. Bell's principles, however, would lead him into further political conflict in his own country, as the Second World War moved towards its conclusion. The Allies had agreed to a policy of 'saturation bombing' in an attempt to drive the Germans towards a surrender. The most brutal British example of this was the attack on Dresden in 1945. Bell was clear what his response to this policy must be, and with great courage he made that response in the House of Lords on more than one occasion. The exchange noted below indicates the unavoidable tensions produced through the need to engage with *prophecy in pursuit of reconciliation*. The exchange is recounted by Bell's old friend Lord Woolton:

> I remember seeing him on the bishops' bench, and I went to him and said, 'George, I believe you are going to make a speech.' He replied, 'Yes, I am.' I said, 'George, there isn't a soul in this house who doesn't wish you wouldn't make the speech you are going to make.' He looked a little downcast at that, and I said, 'You must know that. But I also want to tell you that there isn't a soul who doesn't know that the only reason why you make it, is because you

believe it is your duty to make it as a Christian priest.' That was true: the House held him in the greatest respect, in complete disagreement.[6]

Bell's prophecy, then, was for many deeply unpopular, but it was part of his priestly ministry. The latter part of the twentieth century saw many other examples of such prophecy. Understandably, South Africa during the apartheid era was the focus of much of this. We have already referred to the courageous work of Father Trevor Huddleston CR; much of this is reflected movingly in his own writings.[7] But there was a broader stream of priests and clergy from within all the Christian churches whose prophecy frequently caused them to be expelled for their trouble. The sometime Dean of Johannesburg, Gonville ffrench-Beytagh, was one such. Most famous of all in this conflict was the witness of Archbishop Desmond Tutu, who eventually received the Nobel Peace Prize and later was made Convenor of the 'Truth and Reconciliation' process, following the final collapse of apartheid. In the UK, during the 1950s and 1960s, other Christians felt called to a political witness in opposition to the UK's part in the nuclear arms race. Canon John Collins, of St Paul's Cathedral in London, was effectively the main moving force who brought into being the Campaign for Nuclear Disarmament, which still remains in existence, albeit in a more modest form. These examples – and dozens of others could be given, from around the world – indicate that reconciliation and prophecy are not necessarily in contradiction with each other. Indeed, in certain circumstances, ironically, true reconciliation cannot follow without the conflict necessarily provoked through a prophetic witness. This is itself part of the priestly vocation of the Church.

These two streams running alongside each other remind us that although reconciliation is unquestionably one of the determining features of priesthood within the Christian tradition, it is by no means the only defining element. Michael Ramsey alludes to four main strands. They are the priest as reconciler, as theologian, as a person centred on prayer, and as a priest centred on the Eucharist.[8] As we have already hinted, 'reconciler' includes the priest's role both in politics and in absolution and these are picked up by the archbishop in separate chapters of his classic book. But what of the other three foci? The Eucharist may be a good place to begin. Pivotal within the Eucharist is the moment when we receive Holy Communion. The word 'communion' is crucial in understanding the Eucharist. It is a word used far more richly and widely than in the past in the Church and indeed in theology. So, initially, communion lies at the heart of our understanding of God as Trinity;

the three persons of the Trinity live in perfect communion, thus express-
ing the unity or 'oneness' of God. Mirroring this imperfectly, churches
across the world live in either full or partial communion with each other,
even between different traditions. But the communion we experience
within the Eucharist is both corporately and individually the sign of our
union with God, our Creator and Redeemer. Indeed, the Eucharist is
itself that sacrament which defines the nature of the Church. When
Christian people come together to celebrate the Eucharist, God is there
in their midst and the Church is seen in its fullness, at least on that local
level. The priest focuses this truth in presiding at this great sacrament.
But for the sacrament to be the centre of someone's life means still more
than this. For this refers to the individual priest or lay person being committed to God and the Church through the Eucharist. Not only does
the priest preside at the Eucharist, but the priest's own life is nurtured
through the sacrament and through the communion it manifests. The
priest must be truly eucharistically centred.

Then Ramsey also talks of the priest as *pray-er*. Prayer too must be at
the heart of the priestly life. This is seen to be so already from what we
have said of the Eucharist, but it goes beyond this in such a way that
prayer is interwoven with every aspect of life. Thomas Cranmer, in re-
drawing the pattern of daily prayer for an emerging Church of England,
began with the eight monastic hours of prayer. With extraordinary
facility, and using the English language to the very best of its potential,
Cranmer produced the two daily offices of Morning and Evening Prayer.
His intention had been that these two offices might be pray-able by
laity throughout the Church. Even in Elizabethan times this may have
been expecting more than is realistic, but certainly these two offices have
formed the foundations of daily prayer for the clergy of the Church of
England over the past 450 years. Even now, nearly five centuries later,
one of the requirements for clergy set out in the Canons of the Church
of England remains the saying of Morning and Evening Prayer daily.
There are now other versions of the office from which to choose, but
the aim is still the same. Morning and Evening Prayer (sometimes
called simply Matins and Evensong) frame the priest's day. The day
begins and ends in God, and indeed this sets the scene for all that the
ordained minister is called to do. It frames the lives of those with whom
the priest makes contact too. Prayer and daily life truly become part of
one tapestry.

Even this does not finally exhaust what Michael Ramsey means by
centring one's life on prayer. For alongside the Eucharist and the offices
he commends time for meditation and contemplation. This meant that,

for him, each day would include time for meditative and contemplative prayer, and also periods of retreat throughout the year. Elsewhere in his writings, Ramsey coined a very useful phrase. He talked of 'wasting time with God'. So, when asked, on one occasion, how he used the 30 minutes he put by for contemplative prayer each day, he said it varied: some days he would use it in one particular way, and on other occasions he would try rather different ways into prayer. However, he noted: 'Sometimes I think of everything else in the world for 29 minutes and spend just the last minute in prayer.' That, he reflected, was wasting time with God, but it was time well wasted!

It may seem, initially, quite a long way from wasting time with God, or even from prayer, to theology. But Michael Ramsey and indeed countless others down the centuries have been clear that the priest must also in some sense be a *theologian*. Indeed, far from being an odd starting point, prayer is, in fact, an excellent place from which to begin and set out along this road. Austin Farrer, the great twentieth-century Anglican theologian and preacher, wrote:

> Prayer and dogma are inseparable. They alone can explain each other. Either without the other is meaningless and dead.[9]

These brief sentences introduce a book which is specifically about 'praying the creed'. The creed is a strange mixture between a confession of what we believe, a prayer which takes all of these beliefs into our own consciousness, and, of course, as we noted much earlier on, another way of 'singing the Lord's song' in a strange land. It is unquestionably *theological*. One of the problems we encounter here, however, is that the words 'theology' and 'theologian' are very off-putting, even alarming for many. They seem to describe the work of intellectuals, people sitting in cobwebbed studies writing great tomes. But our reflections so far belie these caricatures. In our discussion of the priest as reconciler we were driven to talk of atonement and redemption and all that that means. Similarly in the previous chapter we explored how Paul understood both redemption and the part which the Church and the ordained minister play in proclaiming that redemption in today's world. But perhaps more than anywhere else, it was in W. H. Vanstone's writings that we saw theology, ministry and prayer issuing as one single activity interwoven together as one seamless garment. In a unique way, Vanstone's writings offer us theology issuing directly from priestly ministry. The stories he tells are all of a piece with his theological reflection upon the priestly life within the places where he served.

Undoubtedly theological reflection can be demanding, and it will be at its most demanding and enriching of all when it emerges from the very ministry in which people are engaged. This process is itself subtle. It requires an initial awareness and comprehension of the Christian tradition as we have received it. That tradition offers us a theological lens through which we can view the world as we encounter it. For Vanstone, the tradition had been so absorbed into himself as to polish that lens very finely. But that polishing process can happen in all of us. What are the materials we need? First of all, the tradition is a given. Second is an increasing sensitivity to the world as we encounter it; what do the relationships and problems which we encounter say about God and God's relationship with our world, both locally and more broadly? Third, we need to nourish the process continually. Prayer, the Eucharist, knowledge of scripture and also sustained reading of both theology and secular literature come together to allow the lens to focus more effectively. Out of this can issue an integrated priestly ministry. Nonetheless, all our reflections on priesthood stand in the context of this ministry not being *our* exclusive possession, nor even that of the Church. For ultimately all ministry is Christ's. Bishop Stephen Bayne, the first Executive Officer of the Anglican Communion, summarizes this very powerfully. He writes:

> . . . there is only one ministry – Christ's ministry. He is the only minister there is in the Church. It is He who receives the baby into His Great Body in baptism; it is He who puts His hands over mine in confirmation or ordination; it is He who stands at the altar and Breaks the Bread . . . because Christ is One and there is only one ministry, then priest and lay people alike need to learn that their separate lives are only two sides of the same coin – that the great imperatives of the Gospel lie over both – that both together must fulfil the work of Christ within the world.[10]

So all human priesthood derives from Christ through his Church. That process of exchange about which we have already spoken is perfectly expressed here. It focuses too that coinherence, theiosis or divinization which describes the possibility of God's divinity permeating our humanity and our humanity returning to the God who created us. This takes us back, then, to the Eucharist where *communion*, that overarching experience linking God and humanity, is most perfectly expressed. The Eucharist is thus transformative of our humanity, allowing it to be lifted up to God. Teilhard de Chardin saw this as a key to understanding the central significance of priesthood in the Church. A recent commentator has summarized his thinking in this way:

> Teilhard regards priesthood, both lay and ordained, as essentially a ministry of eucharistic transformative action. The consecration of the Eucharist which the priest performs represents the transformations which all Christians, in their different types of work, bring to the world, whether in manufacturing, research, service, caring, artistic creativity or other enterprises. This conviction explains Teilhard's arresting representation of the soldiers of the First World War battlefields as priests: they are engaged in a supremely active and sacrificial commission. Teilhard is determined to articulate the importance of human action for the communion of the person with God, portraying it as a kind of eucharistic consecration of that which it touches.[11]

We have seen priesthood, then, from any number of different angles. The determinative image has been that of reconciliation but alongside this have emerged a number of different strands: the priest as *pray-er*, *theologian*, *eucharistically centred* and as simply *being there with people*. All these different strands come together within God's grace forming us into the likeness of Jesus Christ. Through that, God's grace enters our hearts and helps transform us into the likeness of Christ. This process leaves us with just one further image, which in some ways is the most powerful of all. It is crystallized in another saying of Dag Hammarskjöld, whom we mentioned earlier. Hammarskjöld notes:

> In the last analysis it is our conception of death which decides our answer to all the questions that life puts to us.[12]

This realization is taken further in relation to the priesthood by Margaret Craven in her novel about a young priest in the far north-west of Canada, who is terminally ill. Early in the novel, there is this exchange between the bishop and a doctor:

> The doctor said to the Bishop, 'So you see, my Lord, your young ordinand can live no more than three years and doesn't know it. Will you tell him, and what will you do with him?'
> The Bishop said to the doctor, 'Yes, I'll tell him but not yet. If I tell him now, he'll try too hard. How much time has he for an active life?'

'A little less than two years if he's lucky.'

'So short a time to learn so much? It leaves me no choice. I shall send him to my hardest parish. I shall send him to Kingcome on patrol of the Indian villages.'

'Then I hope you will pray for him, my Lord.'

But the Bishop only announced gently that it was where *he* would wish to go if he were young again, and in the ordinand's place.[13]

Towards the end of the book comes the dénouement which indicates what the bishop is about. He is now speaking with the young priest:

'Always when I leave the village,' the Bishop said slowly, 'I try to define what it means to me, why it sends me back to the world refreshed and confident. Always I fail. It is so simple, it is difficult. When I try to put it into words, it comes out as one of those unctuous, over-pious platitudes at which Bishops are expected to excel.'

They both laughed.

'But when I reach here and see the great scar where the inlet side shows its bones, for a moment I know.'

'What, my Lord?'

'That for me it has always been easier here, where only the fundamentals count, to learn what every man must learn in this world.'

'And that, my Lord?'

'Enough of the meaning of life to be ready to die.' And the Bishop motioned Mark to start the motor, and they went on.[14]

So the bishop has sent the young priest there not only to know enough of the meaning of life to be ready to die, but also to help others to learn that meaning too.

This is indeed a profound responsibility, and among all the other roles to which the priest is called could lead both Church and individual priest to an inappropriate hubris or pride. Let us conclude this chapter, then, with two narratives which may be sufficient to undermine any such temptation within any of us. The first narrative acted as the controlling image in an ordination sermon delivered by one of the finest priests of his generation. The preacher began by describing an archaeological dig at the site of the Roman town of Silchester near Reading. Analysis of the dig indicated that the reason for the disappearance of all that Roman fabric beneath a great layer of soil had been through the work of hundreds, thousands and millions of worms over several hundred years. The preacher compared the work of these worms to the tiny contribution that but one priest makes in working with God for the Kingdom of God. He ended: 'So don't expect too much of yourselves, but keep worming away for the Kingdom!' As worms we cannot get above ourselves, but still without that worming far less would be achieved.

The second story is very different and reminds us sharply that vocation is not owned by us, nor is it about a private conversation between each individual and God. Instead, vocation and the discernment of vocation come from outside ourselves. This story takes us back to Palestine, during the Second World War. The chaplain to a battalion in Haifa in Palestine had to visit another battalion under his charge at Port Said in Egypt; he knew he would be gone for a couple of weeks. He briefed his CO and said that everything was in order. The day after the chaplain left, the CO received a call from the bishop. He had decided to come to Haifa, to confirm in a week's time. The CO, determined to put on a good show, detailed six men to be confirmed (the bishop's visit was unexpected!). Duly the bishop came and the men were confirmed. On his return the chaplain asked how things had gone. The CO reported and the chaplain exploded: 'This makes a mockery of all our confirmation training and of Christian teaching.' No more was said, but 20 years on the chaplain received a letter from one of those men who was detailed: 'I thought, sir, that you might be interested to know that I have just been accepted for training for ordination in the Church of England.' The former chaplain replied humbly: 'I'm so pleased. You may be interested to know you're the third of that group to be ordained.'

This true story hardly outlines a perfect process, for if we are called – to baptism, confirmation or ordination – that calling should be affirmed by God's Church as part of a proper process of discernment; and indeed, sacraments do not issue from military orders! Nevertheless, the story does remind us that God's grace works in ways that we may never expect, let alone predict. This calls out of us an appropriate humility both in theology and in our understanding of vocation. That may not be a bad way of leading into our next chapter, which will reflect on service, on the diaconate and on the ministry of deacons. I leave you with another description of the priest's life, which summarizes much of what has gone before:

> To live in the midst of the world without wishing its pleasures;
> to be a member of every family, yet belonging to none;
> to share all sufferings;

to penetrate all secrets;
to heal all wounds;
to go from men and women to God and offer him their prayers;
to return from God to men and women to bring pardon and hope;
to have a heart of fire for charity;
to teach and to pardon, console and bless always,
My God! what a life!
And it is yours, O Priest of Jesus Christ![15]

6

Angels

Deacons as messengers

———◆◆◆———

Back in the 1990s, Robbie Williams' 'Angels' was one of the all-time hits. Some over-zealous teenagers at the time dismissed it as one for grandmas only – but why should the young have all the fun to themselves? In a way this dismissive comment was a back-handed compliment, implying just how popular the song had been. Reflecting on Williams' song, it is difficult to know quite how he feels about angels. He muses about these heavenly beings, wondering whether they may be keeping an eye on him from their privileged and elevated vantage point. Certainly, when it comes to love, angels seem to be very much second-class citizens – they are not his first choice, but instead a substitute for something better – presumably human love. But elsewhere, the feeling in the song is more laudatory, to use an angelic sort of word. There is a hint that angels can even get into the places that our own limited consciousness can never reach.

Moreover, if salvation actually lets their wings unfold, as the song says, then they really are in touch with a higher experience of reality than is open to us. So on the whole the song is welcoming of angels.

What can we say about angels? Well, to begin with we can say that they are more popular than they used to be. This is true both outside and inside the Christian Church. Just a few years back saw angels as rather an embarrassment, little better than the fairies that we know are *not* at the bottom of our gardens. Theologians found them to be deeply embarrassing. Ironically, however, with Renaissance paintings, those depicting angels have frequently been among the most popular of all. Raphael's two cherubs, diminutive heavenly beings, have become almost an icon for a new generation. They gaze out on the universe, ready to pass on a message of goodwill – at least that's what appears to be the case from the looks on their faces. The popularity of Raphael's podgy little fliers, however, seems to have heralded a more general change of heavenly climate. Angels are now increasingly fashionable again.

71

Part of this may be because we are rather more subtle in our interpretation of angels. We are not quite so literalistic. Even so, pictures of
these beings are certainly popular now; a recent exhibition, at Holmfirth
in West Yorkshire, of representations of angels, ranging from fifth-
century Egypt to those painted by the pre-Raphaelites in nineteenth-
century Britain, brought in dozens of visitors throughout the whole of
one summer.[1] South of Newcastle-upon-Tyne, there is even the *Angel of
the North* heralding one's arrival into that part of England. Similarly,
Miss Garnet's Angel, a novel by Salley Vickers, has been extraordinarily
popular in the UK and elsewhere over the past five years or more.[2]
Vickers' novel weaves the story from the Apocrypha of Tobias and the
Angel into the tapestry of her narrative. Without giving too much away
for those who have not read it, the angel, in different ways, transforms
the last years of Miss Garnet's life. She breathes a fuller humanity.

Now at the heart of this changed view of angels is a deeper understanding of what they are about, rather than what they look like, whether
they have wings and whether they are part of the universe that we can
directly apprehend. What is their role? What do they do in each of the
cases we have mentioned? The short answer is that they are *messengers*.
Salley Vickers' angel brings news of a depth to life that Miss Garnet had
never dreamed possible. The Holmfirth angels brought a vitality to a
relatively pleasant but rather ordinary early nineteenth-century church;
it breathed more of the dynamic gospel that caused it to be built. Robbie
Williams' angels again know things that we don't know and they let this
hint of 'something more' spread. They bring a message.

This takes us back to the first telling of the Gospels. In Greek, the word
for gospel is *euaggelion* (in English translated as 'evangelion') which
means simply 'good news' or 'good message'. From the letter to the
Hebrews, which is so good at coining new usages and fresh phrases, we
have those famous lines:

> Let brotherly love continue. Do not neglect to show hospitality to
> strangers, for thereby some have *entertained angels unawares*. [My
> italics. Some translations now put it rather more woodenly: enter-
> tained angels without knowing it.][3]

Here, once again, angels have a message to pass on simply by their
existence. This verse from Hebrews spoke tellingly in earlier days too.

Or, to move to a very different scene: in The Shaven Crown inn at
Shipton-under-Wychwood in Oxfordshire there is a piece of ancient
mediaeval stained glass. It depicts an angel. Why? Because this inn was

once the guesthouse of the (now lost) monastery next door. So, the hospitality in that guesthouse meant that at least one stained-glass angel would be entertained unawares.[4] The concept of angels as messengers, then, is essential in getting the gospel across, both by word and by deed. It has even crept into colloquial language, as if by stealth. When we want someone to do a favour for us, often it will simply be passing a message; we may well encourage the person to do it for us by ending the request with those five simple words. 'Go on, be an angel.'

Now why so much talk about angels, when we are in the midst of a book about vocation, ministry and ordination? Why start with angels when we promised that it would be about deacons? Well, the answer to that is that some of the most recent research suggests that central to the calling of a deacon, or indeed to the calling of a diaconal church, is the role of messenger: from earliest times, deacons were seen as messengers. We shall return to this in a moment. Having spent so much time in heaven, however, and before we return to talk of messengers, let us come down to earth with a bump and ask if there have been any examples of deacons of whom we have heard. They rarely seem to get a mention, and there is an irony here. For deacons can be traced back into the New Testament and the sub-apostolic period (that is, the time of the early Church immediately after the first apostle died); they were an essential part of the Church. Early Byzantine churches almost invariably had a *diakonikon*, a special room for the deacons. Moreover, deacons have a clear and distinct pedigree as an order almost from the beginning. It does not appear to have been until later on that the terms 'priest' and 'bishop' were differentiated. In the sub-apostolic period, 'priest' and 'bishop' appear to have meant the same thing; different churches simply used a different word.

So why did deacons slip out of fashion in some of the mainstream churches – and most notably within Roman Catholicism and Anglicanism? Did no significant individuals remain deacons? The answer is, of course, that they did and probably in significant numbers up until the Middle Ages. Second, although we know the names of few, there are some very important exceptions. So, St Laurence, by tradition said to have been martyred by being roasted on a gridiron in the mid third century, remained a deacon throughout his rather truncated life. St Francis of Assisi, one of the key figures in reforming the Church in the early thirteenth century, was a deacon but never a priest. Nicholas Ferrar, a friend of the great poet, country parson and Caroline Divine, George Herbert, set up a lay community at Little Gidding in Cambridgeshire and lived his whole life in deacon's orders. Each of these also has a strong claim to having lived a diaconal, self-giving life in a most vivid and impressive way. Their whole being reflected that pattern of being which we referred to right back in the introduction, a pattern of being most perfectly modelled in Jesus. It is interesting that the colloquial saying is 'Be an angel.' It does not say do this or don't do that. This highlights something of great significance for one whole theme within vocation and ministry upon which we have not yet focused. It is this question of *being* and it is presented most starkly of all, perhaps, in reflecting on deacons.

One of the complaints often made when people are encouraged to think imaginatively about using the diaconate in a more constructive way is that the deacon cannot *do* any more than a lay person. Everything that a deacon does is already also done by a lay person. Even baptism can be 'done' by a lay person in an emergency. Of course, all of this is true but it can very swiftly take us down a serious and slippery slope. For if we ask that same question about the 'doing' of a priest, even there we get a fairly minimal answer. The only two things that a priest can *do* that others cannot is to preside at the Eucharist and to absolve. If that is all there is to it, then why not get anyone to *do* this where and when it is needed? Indeed, the question is answered in precisely that way by those who argue for 'lay celebration'. Ironically, this strictly functional approach to ministry leads us into difficulties with priesthood if we move in the other direction too. If we are to describe ministry functionally – by doing – then a great deal of what a priest does is diaconal. Indeed, one of the reasons why some priests have reacted negatively, in the past, to a real renewal of the diaconate is that it appears to undermine any distinctive *raison d'être* for their priestly ministry.

But the whole of this line of argument takes us down a blind alley. No one could deny the importance of what a deacon, bishop or priest does. The principle affirmed in the incarnation is one of enfleshing God's presence in the world and that enfleshing means taking seriously the tasks and responsibilities given to us. But it is an error (philosophers call it a 'category mistake' – we have missed the point of the question) to begin with function and doing. First and foremost the Church of God is called to *be* a particular sort of community. It is called to *be* as Christ is in the world, as far as all that is within it allows it to do so. If the Church is called to be that sort of community and to live out that sort of life, then the individual priest, deacon and bishop is similarly so called. It is first and foremost in our *being* that we may be capable of mirroring God. That is why immersing ourselves in the Eucharist and prayer is of such inestimable importance. That offers us the opportunity to be fixed upon the vision of God, as Kenneth Kirk exhorted us, and through that to be unselfed. Such a manner of being will naturally mean that we do different things and that we do things differently because of our transformed *being*.

Interestingly enough, the epistle which is classically chosen for the ordination of deacons makes this point perfectly. The passage that is recommended is the first twelve or thirteen verses of the twelfth chapter of Paul's letter to the Romans. The principle which we have been outlining, and which lies at the very centre of any theology of ordination is there implicitly at the beginning of this passage:

> I appeal to you therefore, brothers and sisters, by the mercies of God, to present your bodies as a living sacrifice, holy and acceptable to God, which is your spiritual worship. Do not be conformed to this world, but be transformed by the renewing of your mind, so that you may discern what is the will of God – what is good and acceptable and perfect.[5]

This is a very rich passage indeed and underpins with great depth and precision what all Christians and so also all ordained ministers are about. First we are challenged to 'present our bodies as a living sacrifice, holy and acceptable to God, which is your spiritual worship'. As Paul uses it here, 'body' refers to the whole of our being. This is precisely the same thing that is implied when, in the Nicene Creed, we talk of the resurrection of 'the body'. This means our whole being. That transformation is effected by God, which is our spiritual worship. The next verse then sets out the nature of this transformation. 'Do not be conformed to this world, but be transformed by the renewing of your mind.' Our nature is taken and accepted by God and then transformed by divine grace. This transformation allows us to discern the will of God – what is good and acceptable and perfect. Having established this key principle in relation to our being, the next verses spell it out lyrically with regard to Christian character. So *doing* does certainly matter but only doing which issues from transformed *being*. This, in other words, establishes in us the character (and for the ordained the charism too) which issues in Christian behaviour. So Paul notes:

> For by the grace given to me I say to everyone among you not to think of yourself more highly than you ought to think, but to think with sober judgement, each according to the measure of faith that God has assigned.[6]

Then, a little later, it is spelt out more precisely still:

> Let love be genuine; hate what is evil, hold fast to what is good; love one another with mutual affection; outdo one another in showing honour. Do not lag in zeal, be ardent in spirit, serve the Lord. Rejoice in hope, be patient in suffering, persevere in prayer. Contribute to the needs of the saints; extend hospitality to strangers.[7]

So many of these challenges we have already set out – prayer, hospitality to strangers, service and community life; the phrase 'contribute to the needs of the saints' means, of course, what we would call stewardship or giving. The 'saints' are the Church; this was the shorthand that was used in apostolic and sub-apostolic times. This last discussion, then, is an essential part of our understanding of both the Church's vocation and our individual representative ministry. It makes sense to look at it within our reflection on deacons and the diaconate, since so much of this underlies the priestly life too. Deacons, bishops and priests are called first in their being; they are effectively *living sacraments*, as they minister to others. Austin Farrer captured this beautifully when talking of priesthood. He wrote:

> So, then, a priest is a living stem, bearing sacraments as its fruits: he gives you the body and blood of Christ: he gives you, if you faithfully confess before him, Christ's own absolution. And that's not all; the man who bears the Sacrament is sacramental himself; he is, one might almost say, himself a walking sacrament. He is the appointed flag for Christ's people to rally round; the centre of unity to which we hold in every place. Just exactly what a priest is, you can see best in the Holy Eucharist. In a great part of that holy action he is, of course, no more than the voice of the congregation. Some of the prayers we say with him, some we let him say for us: it makes little difference. Or again, in receiving the sacrament, the priest is in the same position as any other Christian, receiving the body and blood of Christ. But there is a moment when the priest steps into the place of Christ himself, to do what Christ did, to bless and to break, to present the mysterious sacrifice before God Almighty. It is much the same in absolution . . . These moments, certainly, are exceptional in the activity of a priest; exceptional but still not disconnected with his whole life or character . . . He is always, as I said before, a sort of walking sacrament, a token of

Christ wherever he is: in him Christ sets up the standard of his kingdom and calls us to the colours.[8]

The principle outlined here by Farrer can and indeed must be extended to all three traditional orders of ministry: bishop, deacon and priest. We have seen how these orders reflect the nature of God as is seen in Jesus Christ and that initially they are recognized in the nature of the whole Church. Ordained ministers then focus these qualities in a representative and sacramental way for the whole Church. Diaconal qualities are foundational, since priests and bishops find that an enormous amount of their ministry is essentially diaconal and that this is in itself part of our living out that one ministry which is Christ's, and which Stephen Bayne summarized so well for us in the previous chapter.

Returning now specifically to deacons, we find ourselves looking out on a misty horizon, but in a climate where happily the mist is rising fairly swiftly. The mist has been caused by a lack of focus on deacons in many of the mainstream churches. This situation is, however, changing rapidly in many churches. Reference is often made to the Ecumenical Movement and to the Liturgical Movement, two key developments within the wider Church of God in the twentieth century. Alongside these two developments, there is no doubt that there has emerged, in the past few decades, a 'diaconal movement'. One of the key growth points has been in the Roman Catholic Church, which has since the Second Vatican Council allowed bishops permissively to ordain people whom the Church has described as 'permanent deacons'. Patterns vary between dioceses and between local churches throughout the world. But what might better be described as the distinctive diaconate ('permanent' suggests that a person's vocation can never change) has also begun to emerge in a number of other churches. Deacons are ordained within the Methodist Church in some countries, and also in a number of Reformed churches; the Church of Scotland has an ordained diaconate. Alongside the excellent social work and aid work pursued under the *diakonia* banner, churches within the Lutheran tradition have begun to move towards an ordained diaconate. In some Lutheran churches this already exists and we shall touch on this later. The Scandinavian Lutheran churches are particularly concerned to pursue this avenue and this has been much stimulated through the signing of the Porvoo Declaration, which has brought about organic unity between the Anglican churches of Britain and Ireland and six of the Nordic and Baltic Lutheran churches.

There is quite an irony here, since it is union with Anglican churches that has spurred these developments within Lutheranism, whereas on the whole Anglicans have been either haphazard or even reluctant to embrace a distinctive diaconate. The Episcopal Church in the USA has the most widespread pattern of distinctive diaconate within the Anglican Communion and there is a body of literature which supports this work in America. The Church of England has been most uncertain of all, perhaps, on the diaconate. Three reports have been commissioned in the past 30 years, each coming up with rather different recommendations. The first report, in 1974, recommended the abolition of the diaconate entirely, both transitional and distinctive.[9] The findings of this report were not implemented and once the 'diaconal movement' began to increase in momentum (and across the churches more generally), a second report was published in 1987.[10] This was debated by the General Synod but fell victim to the controversy over the ordination of women to the priesthood; some felt that the report was cynically trying to find a place for women in order that pressure for ordaining women to the priesthood might cease. This was a mistaken impression, but it was sufficient to sideline the report and its recommendations. In 2001, a third report was published for debate in the General Synod.[11] The reason for publishing this third report requires a brief digression, and takes us back to where this chapter began.

Some of the energy for the recovery of a distinctive diaconate in the Episcopal Church of the USA, and for debate in England and elsewhere, had been provided by James Barnett's important book which looked again at the history of the theology of the diaconate.[12] Barnett's scholarship still allowed him to subscribe to a view of the diaconate simply as one of 'humble service'. In 1990, however, John N. Collins reviewed the ancient sources again and arrived at rather different conclusions.[13] His main conclusion was to steer away from 'humble service' towards an interpretation which puts the main emphasis on deacons as *messengers*. While this did not invalidate all the theological analysis of the 1987 Church of England report, it did mean that part of the argument had to be revisited. It has to be said that there is still no final agreement on Collins' research, but that instead there is probably a cautious acceptance of the need for some modification of the earlier position and some embracing of the messenger model.[14] There are moves at the present time also to engage with readers, whose lobby effectively helped sideline the 2001 report. The aim is to see if matters can be moved on, allowing permissive guidelines to support those bishops who wish to ordain to the distinctive diaconate. Bishops are already free to ordain whom they wish, as long as they are prepared to find the costs for training, but legislation would lead to a helpful national structure.

From this debate, initiated by Collins' work and followed up by others, emerge some direction finders. First of all, it is clear the diaconate is foundational; we have seen both here and in earlier chapters how it relates to the ministry of Christ and his self-giving. This also picks up some of the resonances explored by W. H. Vanstone where he talks of God's own self-emptying.[15] This in itself offers hints about the nature of all Christian ministry and particularly that of deacons, and indeed the diaconal ministry of bishops and priests. The emphasis picked up by Collins does not need to collide with earlier understandings, but instead can bring fresh nuances. Frequently 'humble service' has unfortunate and unrealistic overtones. There is a demeaning aspect to such language, bringing before one's mind the self-conscious humility of Charles Dickens' Uriah Heep. The messenger motif and emphasis offer a fresh approach which does not override the foundational sense in which a diaconal, self-giving strand should underlie all ordained ministry. It adds, however, a strong missionary element to the deacon's ministry.

Let us explore that increased missionary strand and then look to some existing examples of deacons who have already risen to this challenge. How might or ought a deacon's ministry evolve? This is a key question since some really fear that ordaining distinctive deacons will further clericalize the Church and lead to a legion of people whom some unkindly label 'sanctuary rats'. By this they mean a group of people who are already turned inwards towards the Church and who would exercise a largely liturgical ministry of a rather esoteric and technical flavour. The true role of a deacon could hardly be farther distanced from this. It is perhaps seen in positive contrast to the ministry of the parish priest. The parish priest has ultimate responsibility locally and administers the parish. With increasing levels of bureaucracy in society and the Church, this inevitably sucks parish priests into a more church-focused ministry. If they try to avoid this, they are in danger of falling away from their responsibilities.

The deacon, however, stands in a rather different position. He or she ought to be able to respond positively to the metaphorical challenge: 'Go on, be an angel.' The deacon should be freed of administrative responsibilities in the parish and be positioned as a 'messenger' who can work on and from the margins. Deacons should be out working in the community in any number of different ways. We shall explore some of these possibilities in a moment. Rooted in the community, the deacon can be a very eloquent example of the Church serving the wider world. Being engaged on the margins, there is also a great likelihood of the deacon identifying people who may be ready either to rediscover the

Christian faith or to discover it for the first time. Starting on the margins, the deacon will be a messenger working with the parish priest, the congregation and the wider community. Oscillating continually between the two milieux, the deacon may be able to bring a new and rather different sort of energy to bear upon the mission of the Church. Deacons will certainly not be stereotyped, since communities, parishes and demographics vary enormously even across apparently similar terrain and cultures.

The sacramental nature of a deacon's ministry will, of course, mean involvement in the liturgy. The traditional roles played by the deacon traditionally need to be exercised imaginatively across the different traditions within the Church. A more constructive approach to intercession could help dovetail the wider missionary work of the deacon into the liturgy. Through preaching, this integration of Church and community might be furthered. It may also be important to involve deacons in the planning of liturgy regularly, so that there is a real engagement between congregation and community. In talking with clergy, it has not been unusual to find that they have had little time to relate to or even know about the industry, commerce and other key activities within the bounds of their parish. As industrial and other specialist chaplaincies become few and far between, and as the traditional model of industrial chaplaincy is increasingly discarded, so deacons may be able to relate to these areas of community life. They may also be able to do so in a manner which is integrative of parish life. Given all these possibilities, then, what examples can we point to already within the diaconate in the UK, or further afield?

Although the history of a distinctive diaconate in the Church of England has been both haphazard and complex, dioceses have still taken their own initiatives. In Portsmouth, since the 1980s and early 1990s, (and later still in Chichester) significant numbers of men and women have been living out an ordained diaconal ministry. In many other dioceses individuals have offered themselves for this ministry and continue to work as deacons in a great variety of different situations. Recently, the diocese of Wakefield has produced a booklet which outlines a vision for the diaconate, seen as a community-based missionary ministry. It is another avenue within which people can offer their lives within the vocation of God's Church.

In a few cases there has even been the possibility of offering for this ministry as a stipendiary minister. Brian, who began as a non-stipendiary deacon, went on to work for the Royal Navy both within administration and also part-time as a chaplain working 'on the edge' of more conventional chaplaincy work. Allen has spent all his ordained life as a stipendiary deacon. Beginning as a curate in a conventional setting, he has spent much of his time as a community health chaplain. This has been an exemplary place from which to exercise a ministry based in the community but still liturgically rooted within the Church. These, then, are two fairly unusual but 'classical' examples of how a stipendiary deacon can help broaden the Church's mission.

Gill too is a stipendiary deacon. Her role is as a Ministry Development Officer within a diocese. Her responsibility is to work with parishes who have developed core group 'ministry teams' to see how this can effectively develop new patterns of mission. Part of that work includes encouraging people to think of offering themselves for some form of public authorized or ordained ministry within God's Church. She also works as a chaplain in a hospice. Kathryn is also a stipendiary deacon. Her role is diocesan-wide, as one of the key people in the development of 'social responsibility'. Here again the work in which she is involved is just the sort of pioneer or frontier ministry which takes her well outside the formal boundaries of the Church. In both these cases it has been this broader imaginative use of ministry that has made it possible for the Church to ordain these two people in a stipendiary role; such opportunities do not abound, but with imagination more may be created.

Roy has had a varied ministry as a deacon and it is difficult to categorize that work as either stipendiary or non-stipendiary. During the first years of his ordained ministry Roy was the senior verger in a cathedral and was paid as such. Later, however, he moved to become chaplain to a diocesan bishop. In making this move some clear historical resonances were being struck, for within the early Christian tradition deacons often tended to work closely with the bishop. Roy had a variety of inter-related roles. He would drive the bishop, look after the bishop's liturgical needs, but also perforce, through the nature of the work itself, find himself engaged with an enormous number of people, many of them well beyond the boundaries of the institutional Church. Now, in retirement, he continues to exercise his diaconal role in yet one more different way, within a parish. Ann has been a parish deacon now for more than 20 years. She works with her husband, who is the parish priest, and she is clear that her ministry is one that takes her out beyond that area of ministry which her husband can reach, because of his ultimate responsibility for the entire parish. Barry is a deacon in what would be described as an 'urban priority area'. The parish lies on the edge of a northern industrial town, which was the centre of the South Yorkshire coalfield. The collapse of deep mining has led to numerous social problems and so to the need for social, economic and spiritual renewal across the whole of the region. The parish church has played a key part in this renewal locally, and as parish deacon Barry plays a key role in working with the wider community. In this case the clergy have no choice but to be deeply engaged with people well beyond the Church. Without such a vision, this church, which is enjoying rebirth, would be isolated from any sense of local community.

These brief cameos offer just some examples of how a variety of people within the Church of England are living out a diaconal call within the broader vocation of the Church. As we hinted earlier this is by no means limited to the Church of England. One other interesting community-based example began some 15 years ago within the Norwegian Lutheran Church. Familiar problems and tragedies were being played out in the streets of Oslo, the Norwegian capital. People were living rough: there were serious problems with drugs and alcoholism. As part of a broader vocation to *diakonia*, the Church decided to ordain deacons to work specifically in this ministry; the Toyenkirchen project was a crucial element in rediscovering the diaconal vocation of the whole Church. They undoubtedly act as messengers, keeping the wider Church engaged with these social issues.

* * *

We began, once again, by recalling a song. Robbie Williams was musing upon the fact that angels have a broader perception than we do about what the future may hold for us. Indeed, there is even a hint of redemption in his song – are they powered by some saving grace? Angels have, perhaps surprisingly, come back into fashion. They are fashionable because they are a vivid way of rediscovering the importance of the messenger. From antiquity we have, as a human community, known the importance of communication both between ourselves and with the transcendent God who always lies ahead of us. The ancient Greeks were keen to write of the life and musings of the gods. One of these gods, Hermes, was himself designated as the messenger. This same process of communication is essential to the Christian life. Opening ourselves to God's grace is the beginning of this in one direction. Offering the treasury of that grace and of the gospel is the *missio Dei*, the mission of God, in which we are all invited to take our part.

Reflection upon deacons and the diaconate has taken us deeper into the vocation into which we are all called. It has reminded us that we communicate the signs of God's Kingdom first and foremost by who we are, through our being 'transformed by the renewing of our minds, so that we may discern what is the will of God – what is good and acceptable and perfect'. This is the ground, the foundation of all ministry and all Christian vocation. It reaches to the ground of our *being*. Maybe you are being nudged: 'Go on, be an angel', or at least a messenger, or even a deacon. Or maybe the nudge is still elsewhere and not necessarily to be a priest or a deacon. Instead, is it a call to preach and teach, or indeed to consider offering yourself within the religious life . . . ?

7

You raise me up

Other vocations: the religious life, readers

—————•◦•—————

> *There is no life – no life without its hunger;*
> *Each restless heart beats so imperfectly;*
> *But when you come and I am filled with wonder,*
> *Sometimes, I think I glimpse eternity.*
>
> *You raise me up, so I can stand on mountains;*
> *You raise me up, to walk on stormy seas;*
> *I am strong, when I am on your shoulders;*
> *You raise me up . . .*
> *To more than I can be.*[1]

Westlife's song hits resonant notes with all of us. Some of these resonant notes have formed part of the melody in the score of our previous chapters. Earlier in the song Westlife hint at times when we are worn down by the cares and problems of life. The presence of just one other person is often sufficient to lift us out of our gloom and self-obsession. Being there with others in times of sorrow and times of joy is part of the Christian life, and part too of Christian ministry. Acting as a 'bridge over troubled water' is one key element in the priestly vocation of God's Church, as we saw. Here, however, the images are rather different; here the spirit is somehow raised up; here persons who offer themselves act almost as sheet anchors or as foundation stones. Sometimes, but not often, we may realize the significance of what we have achieved. In a moment of scientific humility, Sir Isaac Newton, having been praised for his remarkable discoveries, commented:

> I don't know what I may seem to the world, but as to myself, I seem to have been only like a boy playing on the sea shore and diverting myself in now and then finding a smoother pebble or a

prettier shell than ordinary, whilst the great ocean of truth lay all undiscovered before me.[2]

Newton was all too aware that the discovery even of those smoother pebbles or prettier shells owed as much to what he had learnt from others as it did to his own creative instincts and abilities, so elsewhere, in a letter to his fellow scientist Robert Hooke, he wrote:

If I have seen further it is by standing on the shoulders of giants.[3]

It is a similar theme which emerges in our song: 'I am strong, when I am on your shoulders.' This sort of discovery is still more resonant when one finds oneself as part of a wider community of people. Here it is often the case that inspiration, relief and support issue from the rich mixture of talents, abilities and emotional strengths offered within that wider group. Many of the most successful businesses have prospered on account of the talents brought together in this way. The meaning of the word 'university' implies something similar in the realm of education; knowledge is diverse and grows richer when we work in concert with others. Most obviously we see this literally 'played out' in the realm of sport, where the very notion of a team implies as much. Within God's Church this is true *throughout*. So the image of 'singing the Lord's song', captured in Psalm 137, implies that the song was being sung by the entire exiled community of Israel. So too within the Church we have seen that vocation rests with the whole community; the Lord's song is therefore best sung, first and foremost, in choral form and not as a series of disconnected and individualistic solo performances. It is, perhaps, within the religious life that this is most obviously manifested.

In the late 1960s, just after leaving school, a friend and I resolved to meet up, to continue our friendship. He was an undergraduate at the University of Newcastle and so we agreed to regroup in north-east England. He suggested we might spend the weekend at a Franciscan friary. Early in the evening, at the end of a crisp November day, we alighted from the King's Cross–Edinburgh train at Alnmouth station and made our way for about a mile, along the road to the friary. I had never met a friar, a sister or a monk before in my life, let alone stayed at a religious house. Philip was happily already inducted into their ways. We knocked at the door and a friar was silhouetted by a light behind him. He welcomed us in but also informed us that we had arrived during the 'lesser silence' – no talking in corridors or in other public spaces. He took us to supper, which was also silent, and a book was read aloud to all. We talked briefly after supper and then Compline or Night Prayer followed. Then came the 'greater silence' and the friars left for bed with their cowls over their heads. The next day began at 5.30 a.m. when I was awakened by a bang on my cell door and by a brother proclaiming: 'Christ is risen.' My response was certainly not liturgical – I think I said in a sleepy voice: 'Oh, thanks very much.'

For someone so unschooled in the ways of religious communities, this was all very alarming and I began to wonder if I had made a terrible mistake in coming to the friary. The day gradually unfolded with the other 'hours of prayer' (short offices with psalms and readings) and with the Eucharist at midday. As the day wore on I relaxed. The other guests there were an enormously mixed group. They included the then Provost of Newcastle (whom we would now call the Dean), a high-ranking civil servant who had lost his job on account of his alcoholism, a young lad from London who was a heroin addict and who had just completed the detoxification process, an aristocratic young man whose life had been ruined by the onset of a serious psychiatric breakdown, and then, of course, Philip and me. Alnmouth Friary was, at that time, also a Probation Aftercare Hostel and so other assorted guests came and went. By the end of the weekend the experience of staying at the friary had unquestionably transformed my understanding of the Christian life. I had two weeks' holiday ahead of me unplanned and I decided to stay in Alnmouth and at the friary.

What was it that turned my theological and spiritual perceptions upside down? Almost certainly it was a number of things. Here were a group of friars ranging from a novice of about 22 to an elderly man perhaps in his late seventies. They came from an extraordinarily different set of backgrounds. One had taught mathematics in a public school and another was the son of a cabinet minister and stepson of a world-renowned surgeon. Another was formerly a locomotive driver and a great supporter of Derby County, and yet another had been a chartered accountant by profession. Hardly any of the 15 or so friars there at the time had any similar professional experience. But they had one thing in common. Like Francis and his followers, as we encountered them in our second chapter, they had renounced all their possessions and embraced a life of poverty which was to be lived in community. There was more to it still. This common life was interwoven with a rich pattern of prayer. Their commitment to the spiritual life was inescapable. Yet still there was more, for as we have seen, they also lived out the gospel through their own pattern of *diakonia*, serving the world and caring for others. So one evening, young Billy did not return in time for his probation curfew. Something had to be done and Brother Kevin was sent off in pursuit. I agreed to accompany him into the village in search of the young lad. Billy was not a serious criminal; he was effectively a petty thief, the modern equivalent of a small-town sheep-stealer. If, however, he did not return to the friary on time, then the probation order could be lengthened. Seeking Billy out from his girlfriend's home (where he turned out to be) could be one tiny step in breaking the pattern of re-offending which often unnecessarily increases our prison population and ruins a person's life. Brother Kevin knew where he would be and the two of us brought him safely home to the friary.

There is no question of the impact which these two weeks at Alnmouth had upon me. In the words of the song with which we began, there had been a real 'glimpse of eternity'. My vision of the Christian life had been strengthened. My resolve to offer myself in some way began to crystallize more clearly. God's grace, shown through both individuals and the community, had had a powerful effect. I could respond to God in Jesus Christ:

> You raise me up, so I can stand on mountains;
> You raise me up, to walk on stormy seas;
> I am strong, when I am on your shoulders;
> You raise me up . . .
> To more than I can be.

It would be naïve to romanticize the life of that community. Any band of human beings living together will have their stresses and strains. One only needs to reflect upon family life to realize that. Nonetheless, there was something of crucial significance being lived out here. The Franciscans – both Anglican and Roman Catholic – have had a powerful impact upon the Church and the world over many centuries, and still in our own day. Often, as missioners and preachers, their witness has been made broader still. Certainly I owed much of my growing sense of desire to offer for the ordained ministry to their example and to their encouragement. Had I not been engaged to be married, just a few years on, almost certainly I might have tried my vocation with the Society of St Francis.

Out of these reflections, then, two clear patterns emerge. First of all, the nature of the religious life is such that it can teach about and nurture others in the true vocation of God's Church. Living in community and standing well aside from most of the more attractive elements of everyday life offers both a focus for the community and a moving vision to others. It has in itself a 'converting power'. It has had this effect upon so many people at different stages in their lives. Almost 30 years ago now, the journalist Philip Toynbee encountered the women's community at Ty-mawr in the Welsh border country of Monmouthshire. Toynbee came from a well-known intellectual family and he had been quite clear about his rejection of religion and more specifically Christianity. He wrote of the thoughtful scepticism which he had inherited from his parents. His mother did convert to Roman Catholicism soon after his seventeenth birthday, but this further put him off the Christian faith. He reflected:

> From that time until I was fifty-one, and fully equipped with the daunting experiences of adult life, I remained in a fluctuating attitude of hostile fascination toward all forms of religious belief.[4]

His diary tells the story of the dawn of belief in him and his tentative moves towards faith. He recalls:

> One day, for no special reason that I was able to detect, I made what seemed like a final decision that I too believed in God, and was therefore ready to start examining all the religious knowledge I had acquired over the years, not just as an intellectual curiosity but as the possible approach to a living reality.[5]

Integral to this process was Toynbee's engagement with the Society of the Sacred Cross at Ty-mawr. His diary is peppered with references to the community. He writes at one stage:

> Back to Ty-mawr for mass yesterday, after the sisters' annual October holiday from all intruders . . . Being an associate of this holy place gives me an immense satisfaction; the sisterhood of nuns I know; even a growing sense that the Reverend Mother is indeed a true mother to me – though she must be ten years younger.[6]

Toynbee's relationship with the community, then, was a crucial part of the process of his growing into a supple and mature faith. He too had been able to 'glimpse eternity'. His own home, Barn House, became increasingly a community of friends and it may be that his links with Ty-mawr were important here. Whatever the truth may be, it is certainly the case that the community at Ty-mawr was one of the formative influences upon him as he sought to understand more deeply both the nature of the Christian faith and also the vocation of the Church.

Religious communities, however, thrive first and foremost on their own sense of the Church's vocation and their part in that. The sheer variety of communities indicates the different ways in which that vocation may be lived. Franciscan, Benedictine, Cistercian and Ignatian spiritualities are not different gospels. For there is but one gospel, and these different forms of prayer and community life are simply mani-festations of different emphases forming the heart of *one* community's sense of the Christian vocation. Just a brief delve back into history may be helpful here.

In an earlier chapter we touched on the emergence of the religious life. We noted how other religious traditions also include monastic com-munities within their vocation: first-century Judaism was one example, Buddhism another. We also saw how the semi-eremitic (or hermit) life of St Jerome and St Anthony of Egypt itself focused on a central 'con-ventual' church, although the monks continued to live out an individ-ual witness. We mentioned too St Benedict, born in Nursia, in Umbria in Italy, in the late fourth century. Benedict pioneered what is now technically known as the cenobitic – that is, community – life. At his monastery in Subiaco, and more particularly later at Monte Cassino, Benedict pioneered a community-based monastic pattern which he wrote up in his rule. This included groups of ten monks looked after by a dean; this is the root of the Latin word *decanus* and the English translation of this, 'dean'. Within the rule, there was set out a balanced pattern of life under the leadership of the abbot, the 'father' of the community. Essential to the Benedictine life is the practice of listening. The abbot listens to those within the community and thus attempts to gain con-sensus so that the community may live together in harmony. Similarly the monks are bidden to listen to the abbot and to one another. The very first line of the prologue admonishes all within the community:

Listen my son to the instructions of your Master, turn the ear of your heart to the advice of a loving father.[7]

The rule is a practical guide for life, and Benedict, towards the end of his prologue, calls it:

a school for the Lord's service, and in setting it up we hope we shall lay down nothing that that is harsh or hard to bear.[8]

At the very end of the rule he emphasizes once again, in a tentative manner, how his rule is a gentle but ordered way of exploring the monastic vocation:

Wherever you are, then, who are hurrying forward to your heavenly fatherland, do you with Christ's help fulfil this little rule written for beginners . . .[9]

Benedict's pioneering work did not take off immediately. Although both Gregory the Great, who sent Augustine to Canterbury, and Augustine himself were certainly monks, they were probably not Benedictines in quite the way that we would now understand it. It was not until the twelfth century that a community-based monastic life, as we would now recognize it, really began to take off. In 1100, there were about 30 monastic houses in England. By the end of that century there were 300. At the end of the twelfth and the beginning of the thirteenth centuries, communities of mendicant friars emerged following the vision of both St Dominic, who set up the Order of Preachers, and, of course, the three Franciscan orders, following Francis of Assisi. Alongside these orders, other observances were established, often following a stricter version of the Benedictine rule. The Cistercians are one good example of this. At the Reformation, the religious life in the Church of England disappeared, as Henry VIII dissolved the monasteries. In the nineteenth century, however, the religious life was revived and there is now a variety of different communities within the Church of England for both women and men.

In recent years, the pattern of life lived out by Benedictine monks in our contemporary world was made available to a wide audience through the television documentary series *The Monastery*.[10] A group of men from very different backgrounds and experiences agreed to spend time with the Benedictine community at Worth Abbey. The programme gave a clear insight into the pattern of life and prayer called out of those who have chosen to live under the Benedictine rule. Since the nineteenth century, alongside Roman Catholic congregations, numerous Anglican Benedictine communities have grown up, a number of which still continue. So there are men's Benedictine houses at Elmore in Berkshire, Alton in Hampshire and Burford in Oxfordshire. Women Benedictines are also resident at Burford, at Edgware (in outer London) and at

Rempstone in Leicestershire. These are just some of the Benedictine communities still living out the rule within the Church of England, and there are directories which gather together the full range of different houses continuing to live under both Benedict's rule and other rules, some specific to that community alone.[11]

We have already mentioned the Society of St Francis, a Franciscan community for men, in some detail. This is paralleled by the Community of St Francis for women. There is also a Second Order of contemplatives, the Community of St Clare, and a Third Order. The Third Order is similar to some of the communities of oblates attached to other communities. These associateships, oblateships and the Third Order itself are for those who wish to live a disciplined rule of life in association with a specific religious community. The Franciscan Third Order differs from the others in as much as members take life vows which are then renewed annually. In each of these cases, they are open to both clergy and laity, as indeed are the communities themselves. Each is capable of offering others, in the words of our song, the chance to 'glimpse eternity'.

Within the Church of England there has grown up a variety of other communities not living a strictly Benedictine or Franciscan rule, but nevertheless living a rule that has given the order a very distinctive character. So the Community of the Resurrection at Mirfield, founded by Bishops Frere and Gore, has been both missionary (as in the case of someone like Trevor Huddleston) and scholarly; it has continued to run the College of the Resurrection, training men and women for the ordained ministry. The women's Community of the Sisters of the Love of God in Oxford is noted for its life of prayer and for its tradition of teaching the life of prayer. The women's communities of the Order of the Holy Paraclete at Whitby and the Community of St Mary the Virgin at Wantage have had diverse interests in education and mission, but are both rooted firmly in the life of prayer. It is important to mention also the remarkable ecumenical men's community at Taizé, in Burgundy in France, established, after the Second World War, by Brother Roger, Father Max Thurian and others. It is committed specifically to the work of reconciliation between Christians and between nations; there is alongside it a parallel community of sisters living the monastic life close by to the Taizé brothers. These are just a few examples, and it would be tedious to list every community one by one. Indeed we have not listed here other orders who did not live regularly in community. Hopefully these examples, however, alongside the directories, will be sufficient to stimulate the reader to consider this essential way of living out the vocation of God's Church. God's Church would be much the poorer without religious communities contributing to its life.

The religious life, then, is once again a very specific way of focusing certain aspects of the vocation of the whole Church. In *The Vision of God*,[12] to which we pointed earlier, Kenneth Kirk makes it clear that the monastic life, in all its different forms, is not a *better* way of living out the Church's vocation than is living the Christian life in the world; it is different. There is, in other words, no 'double standard' in Christianity. We are all called to fix our eyes on the vision of God and allow ourselves to be 'unselfed' in whatever manner of life we find ourselves called to live. Those called to be friars, sisters or monks are focusing specific aspects of the Christian life and vocation for us all. As we saw a priest, a bishop or a deacon focusing aspects of life in God, so too do those called to the religious life. There is a sense in which they vicariously live for us the life of prayer, contemplation, *diakonia* or specific calls to mission. Nonetheless, we are all called to play our part in these aspects of the Church's vocation alongside religious. Returning to the song with which we began, we are all called to 'raise others up', to strengthen them in faith, and to be beacons of the gospel ourselves. We have seen how religious communities do this in a very particular way.

We began with my experience in encountering the Society of St Francis back in the late 1960s. One generation on saw my younger son studying theology at university. It happened that his tutor had strong links with the Order of St Benedict at Burford. She knew that the brothers and sisters there were soon to organize a 'painting week'. She encouraged some of her students to think of taking part. Now this was no class for aspiring Rembrandts or Raphaels. Instead it was a week when volunteers could stay at the priory and contribute to the life of the community by helping with painting and maintenance. My son went with others to help. Some were older and already had links with the community. My son was unquestionably profoundly affected by the experience. But this time it was not an active community like the Franciscans whom I had encountered at Alnmouth, but instead an order dedicated to the life of prayer and rooted in the vow of *stability*. Alongside this vow, however, runs another commitment which requires the sisters and brothers to greet every guest 'as if he or she were Christ'. This vow of hospitality, alongside the life of prayer, helped convince my son that he should offer himself for ordination. He is indeed now a priest.

So, once again, a religious community had 'raised someone up', encouraging them to offer themselves for the ministry of God's Church.

There is no life – no life without its hunger;
Each restless heart beats so imperfectly;
But when you come and I am filled with wonder,
Sometimes, I think I glimpse eternity.

As with most popular music, the theme here is romantic love, but in this verse the resonance can be transferred fairly directly to Christian faith and the love of God. God's grace, working through others, can help nourish our hunger for the divine spirit. God can raise us up, and does so through the company, ministry and sacramental lives of other women and men. Religious communities have the power to do this in a particularly resonant manner. Time with a religious community has, in the case of two of us – from quite different generations – helped us glimpse eternity. But more than this, we may be caught up into the vision which the community itself represents. We may be called to be religious – that is, monks, sisters or friars. The Church of God has been enriched by the religious life over two millennia and the call of that life remains as strong as ever. Might you find yourself called to live out the gospel in community, either actively or as a contemplative? If not, are you called to an associateship or as part of the Franciscan Third Order? These callings also strengthen the focus of prayer and can help structure our own lives. It is often a subtle and complex process of discernment which helps us to identify our own part in the vocation of God's Church. Not everyone will be called to the religious life, nor indeed to the ordained ministry, within or outside a religious community. It may be that instead the essential element of our call will be as a lay person, but nevertheless a lay person with a specific role in worship or teaching. Might that mean offering oneself for selection as a reader? How might we begin to explore what this means?

* * *

Perversely, perhaps, let us begin with developments in our cathedral communities. Over the past 50 years, there have been two significant parliamentary measures aimed at helping cathedrals develop their ministry appropriately, in the context of contemporary society.[13] One notable development in the light of this has been the appointment of lay canons. In some dioceses the lay canons have been appointed to signal their remarkable achievements in their own field, at the same time as being committed members of the Church of England. So among these lay canons we encounter Emma Bridgewater, the first person to set up a new commercial 'designer' pottery in Staffordshire in recent years. Or there is Professor Philip Wilby, formerly professor of music at the University of Leeds, and also a leading composer of contemporary church music. Then again there is Juliet Barker, the author of the most distinguished study of the Brontë family and their achievements. There are other equally interesting examples including Stanley Innis, a chairman of employment tribunals and a leading individual working with minority ethnic communities; Stanley comes himself from the West Indies originally. All these people are committed to their lay status, but through their own talent and expertise have shown how the Church's vocation extends into all aspects of human life. People can 'be raised up' by God's grace through work in the arts, in business, in literature and in public life.

In contrast to these, there is another group of lay people who feel that they may have something to offer as teachers within the Church, and as preachers within the liturgy, while still being clear about not wishing to be ordained. Earlier on, we set out the origins of reader ministry within the Church of England and we do not need to add to this here. Again, this is a public and representative ministry which focuses one key part of the Church's educational and liturgical vocation. Also, once again, people with distinguished careers in other walks of life may find themselves called to be a reader alongside their secular vocation. So there are television producers, judges, religious brethren, business executives, professional theologians – all offering this ministry alongside the other work; the present Secretary-General of the General Synod of the Church of England is himself a reader. Given the necessary educational base, however, reader ministry is open to people from every conceivable part of society: farmers, those working in industry, commerce and local government, doctors and nurses – anyone may be called to minister in this way. All these people will also be called to 'raise people up' in the gospel, and most notably, in teaching the gospel and its application for our world. We are, then, enriched by receiving the wisdom of others through God's grace:

> I am strong, when I am on your shoulders.
> You raise me up . . .
> To more than I can be.

If the tradition, beginning with Jesus, lived by the apostles and 'once delivered to the saints' is to be nurtured and handed on, then there is an essential need for those people who, alongside ordained clergy, will offer their gifts as teachers and preachers.

Sometimes, admittedly in a small minority of cases, reader ministry will be 'transitional'. People will offer themselves for training as readers. They will so minister, but then later decide that they are being drawn to offer their talents and abilities in the ordained ministry. Many years ago now, even before I reached my twenties, I offered myself for reader training and was accepted. At the tender age of 22, I was licensed by the Bishop of London in the Church of St Lawrence Jewry, next to the Guildhall. I worked as a reader for some five years before I was ordained. Nevertheless the process of discernment turned out to be twofold. First I felt called to train as a reader, and then some five years later was convinced that I should offer myself for possible selection for ordination training. Readers offer an immensely important and distinctive ministry in all parts of the Church. It is not a replacement for, or pale imitation of, the ordained ministry. Instead it is a distinctively lay role within the Church which contributes an essential part within the liturgical and educational ministry of the Church. At the present time, we are just beginning to become more discerning in distinguishing effectively between the sacramental and missionary ministry of deacons and the teaching and preaching ministry of readers. Both these roles may bring with them clear elements of pastoral work, but the essence of these two ministries is as outlined above. The questions which challenge us are: do you see yourself as a possible teacher and preacher? Do you feel that you will offer your own contribution most effectively as a lay person; working with God's grace? Will you most effectively help to raise others up through the representative lay ministry of the reader?

* * *

We may appear to have moved an enormous distance. We began in Alnmouth Friary with a group of brothers within life-vows, committed to life in community and wearing the distinctive habit based on that worn by Francis himself. We touched too on other communities committed even more single-mindedly to the life of prayer. The Community of St Clare, for example, is an *enclosed* community from which the sisters rarely emerge, save for practical matters which inevitably draw them out for one official reason or another. Their intention is to live a life of prayer, given to God, and on behalf of the Church. This is far from a wasted life. It is but one more example of people offering themselves so that they (and in this case the community as a whole) can be offered as a focus of one element within the total calling of God's Church. But then we concluded with readers, almost all of whom are not just committed to a lay witness, but also to offering that witness *within the everyday life of the contemporary world.* What could there be in common here?

The answer is, of course, that each of these distinctive offerings – and 'offering' is the key word – helps focus for the Church and for the world the *vocation* of God's Church. Through a life dedicated in these different ways, people can be drawn to the pattern of life lived out classically and uniquely in Jesus Christ. This is at the heart of the gospel, for as Archbishop Michael Ramsey reminded us, 'God is Christlike, and in God there is no un-Christlikeness at all.' It is then the one ministry of Christ which all of us share – lay people, deacons, bishops, priests, readers, friars, sisters and monks. It is Christ who can make us all sing the Lord's song. We can sing together, not as a popular song, but as a hymn to God the Father through our Lord Jesus Christ:

> You raise me up, so I can stand on mountains;
> You raise me up, to walk on stormy seas;
> I am strong, when I am on your shoulders;
> You raise me up . . .
> To more than I can be.

Coda

Offering, worship, Eucharist, contemplation, silence

Many of the most interesting pieces of music finish with a brief tailpiece, a coda. Sometimes it offers one more new idea. More often, however, it picks up themes already played and gives them one final interesting twist. Maybe just a brief coda will be useful in completing our musical composition, our singing of the Lord's song in this strange land. To set us off there is one more song. This song, however, was not a number one hit at some point in the last 50 years. Indeed, it was never a number one hit. It may instead qualify as one of the oldest songs to emerge from the land which we now know as England. It is written by Caedmon, arguably the earliest English poet, who worked at the monastery at Whitby and who died in the late seventh century. It was preserved for us by Bede in his *Ecclesiastical History of the English People*:

> Praise now the maker of the heavenly kingdom
> the power and purpose of our Creator,
> the deeds of the father of glory.
> Let us sing how the eternal God,
>   author of all miracles,
> first created the heavens for the sons of men
>   as a roof to shelter them.
> And how their almighty Preserver gave them
>   The earth to live in.[1]

Caedmon's message, then, is that, before all else, we are called to praise God. His main theme is that we should praise God for creation. But towards the end of his song he talks too of God as Preserver. God brings things into being; he also sustains them, and as we have seen has redeemed all that which needs redemption. All this we receive through

God's grace; we receive it as an entirely free gift. None of it is deserved, we have not worked for it as a reward. We receive it entirely gratuitously. God pours this forth from the generosity of divine Being. This, then, is indeed cause for praise. It suggests, too, that perhaps the very first element which we can identify in the Church's vocation is the call to praise and thanksgiving. Addison's great hymn captures it perfectly:

> When all thy mercies, O my God,
> My rising soul surveys.
> Transported with the view I'm lost
> In wonder, love and praise.

And then later:

> Through all eternity to thee
> A joyful song I'll raise
> But, oh, eternity's too short,
> To utter all thy praise.

Praise, then, is the beginning and ending of the vocation of God's Church and into that is caught up the offering of all who would minister.

Throughout these reflections, we have encountered time and again the call to prayer, to the Eucharist, to silence and to contemplation. As we saw, none of this drives from us the need for intellectual honesty and intelligence about our faith. Michael Ramsey reminded us that the priest should also be a theologian. That is true of all caught up in ministry, but it should be true in a slightly different way for *all* believers. Scripture reminds us that we should be capable of giving an account of the faith that is in us. St Anselm reminded us too that we should live a faith which seeks understanding. But all this takes place within the context of praise. That was part of what Austin Farrer was telling us when he insisted that prayer and theology should never be allowed to drift apart from each other.[2] So a theme that has arisen again and again, rather like a rondo – to continue the musical theme – is that of prayer, silence, contemplation and the Eucharist. Not only are these the first and natural responses to God's grace and God's abounding generosity in all that we receive freely, they are also a challenging witness to the world. We live in a world of noise rather than silence, a world of busy-ness rather than contemplation, a world of preoccupation rather than prayer, and in a world of sadness rather than thanksgiving and celebration – to pick up themes which go to the root of the meaning of the Eucharist. Ministers witnessing to each of these will touch hearts more swiftly even than they will by their actions.

Some years ago, in one of those thought-pieces from *The Times*, published on a Saturday, Janet Martin Soskice mused upon the way we often introduce people to our cathedrals, abbeys and great churches. She focused, in this case, on the Church of St Anastasia in Verona. With great sensitivity she interprets two frescoes, one of Jesus being baptized by John the Baptist and the other of the resurrection. Both paintings are about new life, she continues. Then she focuses on the leaflet she has collected at the door. She notes:

> Of this profound theological image [new life] that leaflet tells us only that the baptism is attributed to Jacopino di Francesco, an early 14th century painter from Bologna and one of the founding fathers of painting in the Po Valley. *Finis*. Not even a mention of the resurrection. This is information for the short-term memory, a constantly fed, continuously dissolving fact heap.
>
> The tourists turn away. No one is telling them what to see as they look, and in this the religious authorities seem to collude – indeed they may well have written the leaflets.

So what might the appropriate response and interpretative assistance have been if the Church really got underneath the imagery and religious consciousness which caused those stunning frescoes to be painted? Soskice is quite clear, and she concludes:

> Yet despite neglect and ignorance, gently shining forth for those who look is the life of the building, a life given to it by masons and painters and by those who have prayed in it over hundreds of years, a living breath that whispers in stone, or paint, or light – 'Glory, Glory.' We must try to see *that* [my italics].[3]

This brief reflection can speak volumes to those of us who are ordained, or are thinking that we might offer ourselves in service to God our Creator and to our fellow men and women in this way. Janet Soskice is pointing to the almost sacramental nature of those frescoes. Like an icon, frescoes, sculpture and all forms of Christian art can focus our devotion and lead us on to the God for whose glory this religious art has been produced. If, as Austin Farrer suggests, those who are ordained are effectively 'walking sacraments', then our commitment to the life of prayer and to the Eucharist will be an essential part of the ordained life. Even our lives will be to a degree iconic, not unlike those frescoes; both the Book of Common Prayer and *Common Worship* ordinals make this point as they describe the role of the priest; it is also there implicitly within the ordination prayer itself. In a series of what were effectively 'review articles' in *The Times* newspaper in 1979, Bernard Levin made this very point. In reviewing a book by Gai Eaton, *King of the Castle*, he wrote:

> For him [Mr Eaton] as for Mr Bolton [the writer of the book reviewed the previous day], man is God's viceroy on earth with this difference from more temporal viceroys; that his viceregal role is forever autonomous, with no need or opportunity to refer back to home government for instructions.

Levin concludes by quoting Mr Eaton fairly extensively:

> Standing, as it were, at the pavement's edge with his tray of goods, the priest reduces the price until he is offering his wares for nothing: divine judgement is a myth, hell is a wicked superstition, prayer less important than decent behaviour and God himself dispensable in the last resort: and still the passers-by go their way, sorry over having to ignore such a nice man but with more important matters demanding their attention. And yet these matters with which they are most urgently concerned are, for so many of them, quicksands in which they feel themselves trapped. Had they been offered a real alternative, a rock firm planted from the beginning of time, they might have been prepared to pay a high price.
>
> It is even possible that, had the priest turned his back upon them, attending only to the divine sun which seizes and holds his gaze, they might have come up quietly behind him, knelt down – looking where he looks – and forgotten all their care, all their troubles. It might be said that the basic command of religion is not 'Do this!' or 'Do not do that!' but simply 'Look!' The rest follows.[4]

Now we may want to avoid some of that rant at the start of the quotation, and we would certainly want to avoid falling into the trap which might provoke such criticisms. But the thrust of what is being said there captures the precise intention of this tiny coda, and collects together obliquely some of the other themes of this book. It is our *being* that will first help transform others. That being itself will be transformed by our staying our hearts upon the *vision of God* in Jesus, as Kenneth Kirk suggested, and as is hinted at in that piece just quoted. All this will only be possible if our hearts are caught up into the 'praise of the maker of the heavenly kingdom . . . transported and lost in wonder, love and praise'. That may attract others to come up and quietly kneel behind us as we say 'Look' and they catch a glimpse of all that whispers 'Glory, Glory.'

Notes

Introduction

In a number of the books and articles quoted the language is not inclusive. I have quoted the material as it was written but the reader may wish to 'inclusivize' the language. In some instances this may raise theological issues and different readers will respond differently at those points.

1 Both sides, now

1. 'Both sides, now', words and music by Joni Mitchell © 1967 (renewed) Crazy Crow Music. All rights administered by Sony/ATV Music Publishing, 8 Music Square West, Nashville, TN 37203. All rights reserved. Used by permission.
2. Cf. William Dalrymple, *From the Holy Mountain* (London, Flamingo, 1998).
3. Cf. Alan Bullock, *Hitler and Stalin: Parallel Lives* (London, HarperCollins, 1991).
4. Jung Chang and Jon Holliday, *Mao: The Unknown Story* (London, Vintage, 2006).
5. Thomas Hardy, 'The Convergence of the Twain' in *Collected Poems* (London, Macmillan, 1976), p. 307.
6. Max Ehrmann, 'Desiderata'.
7. *Hamlet*, act 1, scene 2.
8. Cf. Mark Tully, *Something Understood* (London, Hodder and Stoughton, 2001), p. 27.
9. Romans 7.14–21, RSV.
10. William Wordsworth, 'Ode: Intimations of Immortality from Recollections of Early Childhood'.
11. Michael Mayne, *Enduring Melody* (London, Darton, Longman and Todd, 2006).
12. Edwin Muir, 'The Child Dying', *Collected Poems* (London, Faber, 1976), p. 178. By permission of Oxford University Press, Inc.
13. Edwin Muir, 'One Foot in Eden', *Collected Poems*, p. 227. By permission of Oxford University Press, Inc.
14. W. H. Vanstone, *Love's Endeavour, Love's Expense* (London, Darton, Longman and Todd, 1977).
15. Owen Chadwick, *The Secularisation of the European Mind in the Nineteenth Century* (Cambridge, Cambridge University Press, 1975), p. 258.

2 American pie

1. Don McLean, 'American pie' (Universal Music Publishing).
2. David Jasper, *Coleridge as Poet and Religious Thinker* (London, Macmillan, 1985), p. 53.

3 Quoted in Jasper, *Coleridge as Poet*, p. 52.
4 *The Rime of the Ancient Mariner*, Part VII, lines 514–19.
5 Dag Hammarskjöld, *Markings* (London, Faber and Faber, 1964), p. 85.
6 'American pie'.
7 Peter Berger, *A Rumour of Angels* (London, Penguin, 1969).
8 Trevor Huddleston, *Naught for Your Comfort* (London, Collins, 1956).
9 Alan Paton, *Cry, the Beloved Country* (Harmondsworth, Penguin, 1958).
10 Isaiah 5.8, AV.
11 Paton, *Cry, the Beloved Country*, p. 72.
12 Quoted with the kind permission of the author.
13 Ludwig Wittgenstein, *Tractatus Logico-Philosophicus* (Cambridge, Cambridge University Press, 1921), 6.44.
14 Quoted in Mark Tully, *Something Understood* (London, Hodder and Stoughton, 2001), p. 27.

3 Imagine

1 John Lennon, 'Imagine' (Lenono Music).
2 Matthew 6.34, RSV.
3 Matthew 5.48, RSV.
4 *Memorials and Correspondence of Charles James Fox* (London, 1854), Vol. II, p. 361.
5 Quoted in Conor Cruise O'Brien, *The Great Melody: A Thematic Biography of Edmund Burke* (London, Sinclair-Stevenson, 1992), p. 387.
6 Cf. William Hague, *William Pitt the Younger* (London, HarperCollins, 2004).
7 Cf. her novels, especially *The Sea, The Sea, The Bell* and *The Green Knight*, and also, among her philosophical writings, *The Sovereignty of Good* (London, Routledge and Kegan Paul, 1970).
8 Kenneth Kirk, *The Vision of God* (abridged edition – but the original Bampton Lectures in the University of Oxford, 1928; Cambridge, James Clarke, 1977), p. 25.
9 Kirk, *Vision of God*, p. 46 (his italics).
10 Matthew 5.48, RSV.
11 *The Franciscan*, Vol. XIV, No. 2 (March 1972).
12 A. M. Ramsey, *God, Christ and the World* (London, SCM Press, 1969), pp. 99–100.
13 Notes from unpublished lecture to the Anglo-Scandinavian Theological Conference in Lincoln in 1979.
14 Philippians 2.5–8, RSV.
15 Quoted in John V. Taylor, *The Christlike God* (London, SCM Press, 1992), p. 242.
16 Taylor, *The Christlike God*, p. 273.

4 The way old friends do

1 Benny Andersson and Björn Ulvaeus, 'The way old friends do' (Andersson/ Ulvaeus BOCU Music Ltd). Reproduced by kind permission of BOCU Music Ltd.

2 William Shakespeare, *The Merchant of Venice*, act 3, scene 1.

3 Romans 7.15, 18, NRSV.

4 Cf. Romans 4.

5 Romans 5.15, 18, NRSV.

6 2 Corinthians 5.16–20a, NRSV.

7 1 Corinthians 4.1, NRSV.

8 Stevie Smith, 'The Airy Christ', *Collected Poems* (London, Allen Lane, 1975), p. 345. Reproduced by kind permission of the Executors of James MacGibbon's estate.

9 W. H. Vanstone, *The Stature of Waiting* (London, Darton, Longman and Todd, 1982), pp. 67–8.

10 John 4.1–42.

11 2 Corinthians 5.19.

12 Eric James (ed.), *Stewards of the Mysteries of God* (London, Darton, Longman and Todd, 1979). See the essay by Helen Oppenheimer, 'Ministry and priest-hood', especially p. 11.

13 Acts 6.2.

14 Cf. John N. Collins, *Diakonia: Reinterpreting the Ancient Sources* (New York and Oxford, Oxford University Press, 1990).

15 See Avery Dulles' classical analysis of this in his *Models of the Church* (New York, Bantam, 2000).

16 See my 'Mirroring God' in *Theology*, Vol. LXXXVIII, No. 726 (November 1985), pp. 453–60, but note that I would now make it clear that the pattern must be: God – Church – ordained minister.

17 See, for example, the Franciscan Third Order.

18 Quoted in one of the biennial meetings of senior leaders of the Church of England and the Church of Scotland – both established churches.

19 Bernard Levin, 'Faith and the fainthearts', *The Times*, 17 August 1988.

5 Bridge over troubled water

1 Romans 12.14–15, NRSV.

2 Romans 5.18, NRSV.

3 See Paul Fiddes, *Past Event and Present Salvation* (London, Darton, Longman and Todd, 1989), which gives an excellent summary and critique of these theories alongside another concept which tries to hold together the best elements of a number of these theories.

4 This model is set out in more detail in Stephen Platten and John Sharpe, 'Christ – holding humanity in God?' *Theology*, Vol. XCII, No. 746 (March 1989), pp. 113–20. This approach does bring together in one model a pattern which works for both the individual and humanity as a whole.

5 W. H. Vanstone, *Love's Endeavour, Love's Expense* (London, Darton, Longman and Todd, 1977), p. 62.

6 Ronald C. D. Jasper. *George Bell: Bishop of Chichester* (London, Oxford University Press), p. 277.

7 See particularly, once again, Trevor Huddleston, *Naught for Your Comfort* (London, Collins, 1956).

8 A. M. Ramsey, *The Christian Priest Today* (London, SPCK, 1972; 2nd edn, 1985).
9 Austin Farrer, *Lord I Believe* (London, SPCK, 1962), p. 9.
10 Stephen Bayne, *Now is the Acceptable Time* (Cincinnati, Forward Movement Publications, 1983), p. 79.
11 David Grumett, 'The eucharistic cosmology of Teilhard de Chardin', *Theology*, Vol. CX, No. 853 (January–February 2007), p. 28.
12 Dag Hammarskjöld, *Markings* (London, Faber and Faber, 1964), p. 136.
13 Margaret Craven, *I Heard the Owl Call My Name* (London, Picador, 1976), p. 3.
14 Craven, *I Heard the Owl*, p. 119.
15 Michel Quoist, *Prayers of Life* (Dublin, Gill and Macmillan, 1965), p. 51.

6 Angels

1 Celia Kilner, a professional sculptress, painted copies of dozens of different portraits of angels for the exhibition *Angels*, which started its tour around England in Holmfirth Parish Church in Yorkshire.
2 Salley Vickers, *Miss Garnet's Angel* (London, HarperCollins, 2000).
3 Hebrews 13.1–2, RSV.
4 The inn's name, The Shaven Crown, refers to the tonsured monks who lived in the nearby monastery.
5 Romans 12.1–2, NRSV.
6 Romans 12.3, NRSV.
7 Romans 12.9–13, NRSV.
8 Austin Farrer, 'Walking sacraments' in J. L. Holden (ed.), *A Celebration of Faith* (London, SPCK, 1970), pp. 109–10.
9 *Deacons in the Church* (London, Church Information Office, 1974).
10 *Deacons in the Ministry of the Church* (London, Church House Publishing, 1987).
11 *For Such a Time As This* (London, Church House Publishing, 2001).
12 James Monroe Barnett, *The Diaconate: A Full and Equal Order* (New York, Seabury Press, 1981).
13 John N. Collins, *Diakonia: Reinterpreting the Ancient Sources* (New York and Oxford, Oxford University Press, 1990).
14 There is an excellent critical review of this discussion in Paula Gooder, '*Diakonia* in the New Testament: A Dialogue with John N. Collins', *Ecclesiology*, Vol. 3, No. 1 (2006), pp. 33–56.
15 W. H. Vanstone, *Love's Endeavour, Love's Expense* (London, Darton, Longman and Todd, 1977).

7 You raise me up

1 Brendan Graham and Rolf Lovland, 'You raise me up'.
2 Quoted in Joseph Spence, *Observations, Anecdotes and Characters of Books and Men, Collected from Conversation*, ed. J. Osborn (Oxford, Clarendon Press, 1966).

3 Letter to Robert Hooke, 5 February 1676, in H. W. Turnbull (ed.) *Correspondence of Isaac Newton*, vol. 2 (Cambridge, Cambridge University Press, 1960), p. 437.

4 Philip Toynbee, *Part of a Journey* (London, Collins, 1981), Preface, p. 9.

5 Toynbee, *Part of a Journey*, pp. 10–11.

6 Toynbee, *Part of a Journey*, pp. 54 and 55.

7 Dom David Parry OSB (ed.), *The Rule of St Benedict* (Leominster, Gracewing, 1990), p. 1.

8 Parry, *The Rule of St Benedict*, p. 4.

9 Parry, *The Rule of St Benedict*, p. 118.

10 *The Monastery*. Shown on BBC2 in May and September 2005.

11 The most comprehensive directory, published biannually, is *The Anglican Religious Communities Yearbook* which includes communities across the Anglican Commission. The most recent edition at the time of writing is the 2006–7 edition (Norwich, Canterbury Press, 2005).

12 Kenneth Kirk, *The Vision of God* (London, Longman Green, 1934, and Cambridge, James Clarke, 1977).

13 See The Cathedrals Measure 1963 and The Cathedrals Measure 1999.

Coda

1 Cf. Bede, *Ecclesiastical History of the English People* (London, Penguin Classics, 1990).

2 Austin Farrer, *Lord I Believe* (London, SPCK, 1962).

3 Janet Martin Soskice, 'Churches must help tourists to see as well as to look', 'Credo', *The Times*, 26 May 2001.

4 Bernard Levin, 'If hell is your choice choose it', *The Times*, 1979.

Index

Abba 41, 42, 43
absolution 59, 63; *see also* atonement; reconciliation; sacrament of penance
Addison, Joseph 98
AIDS (Africa) 3, 21
Alnmouth Friary, visit to *see* Franciscans
ambiguity 1–2, 3, 5–10, 13
'American pie' 14–27; *see also* Holly, Buddy; McLean, Don
Andersson, Benny 103
Angel of the North 72
angels 71–83; as messengers 73–4
'Angels' (Robbie Williams song) 71
Anglicanism 13, 24, 49–51; in Australia 50; Episcopal Church of the United States of America 78; *see also* Church of England
Anselm, St 98; *see also* Canterbury, Archbishops of
Anthony of Egypt, St 52, 89
anti-clericalism *see* French Revolution
apartheid *see* South Africa
Aquinas, St Thomas 52
Armenian genocide 3
Assisi *see* Francis, St
atonement: through Jesus 58–9, 61; *see also* priesthood; reconciliation
Augustine of Hippo, St xi
'Auld lang syne' *see* New Year's Eve

Balfour Declaration 28
Barmen Declaration (Adolf Hitler) 62
Barnett, James Monroe 78, 105
Bayne, Bishop Stephen 66, 77, 105
Beatles xiv, 17
Bede, the Venerable 97, 106; *Ecclesiastical History of the English People* 97
'being' and 'doing' 74–5

Bell, Bishop George 62–3; parliamentary speech against bombing of Dresden 62
Benedict 52, 89–91; Monte Cassino 89; rule of 89–91
Benedictine Anglican communities: Alton 90; Burford 92; Edgware 90; Elmore 91; Rempstone 91
Benedictines xiii, 52, 89–91
Berger, Peter 19, 103
Berlin Wall 19; breaching of 24
bishops 51, 74, 76–8; focus of unity 51; as 'living sacraments' 76
Bonhoeffer, Dietrich (Confessing Church) 62
Book of Common Prayer 100
'Both sides, now' 1–13, 102; *see also* Mitchell, Joni
'Bridge over troubled water' 56–70; *see also* Simon and Garfunkel
bridges, as icons of modern engineering 56; image of 56
Brother Roger *see* Taizé Community
Buerk, Michael *see* Ethiopia
Bullock, Alan 102
Burford, Order of St Benedict *see* Benedictine Anglican communities; communities, religious
Burke, Edmund 31–2; *Reflections on the Revolution in France* 32

Caedmon 97
Campaign for Nuclear Disarmament 63
'Candle in the wind' (Elton John) 22
Canterbury, Archbishops of: Michael Ramsey 36–7; Robert Runcie 50; Rowan Williams 22–3, 26; St Anselm 52
Caroline Divines 36
Castro, Fidel (Cuban Missile Crisis) 18; *see also* Soviet Union

Chadwick, Owen 11–12, 61, 102
Chang, Jung 102
Chesterton, G. K. 25; 'Ballad of the White Horse' 25
Christianity 34–40
Church of England 50, 80, 82; as established Church 53–4; Morning and Evening Prayer 64; reader ministry in 53; *see also* bishops; communities, religious; deacons; Ecumenical Movement; Franciscans; Liturgical Movement; ordination; priests
Cistercians xiii, 90
Cluniacs xiii
Coleridge, Samuel Taylor 7, 15–16, 103; *The Rime of the Ancient Mariner* 15–16
College of the Resurrection 91; *see also* communities, religious (Mirfield)
Collins, Canon John *see* Campaign for Nuclear Disarmament
Collins, John N. 78–9, 104, 105
Common Worship 100
communion *see* Eucharist
communities, apostolic xiii
communities, religious: Order of the Holy Paraclete, Whitby 91; Order of St Benedict, Burford 92; the Resurrection, Mirfield 91; St Clare 21, 91, 95; St Francis 91; St Mary the Virgin, Wantage 91; Sant'Egidio 21, 48; Sisters of the Love of God, Oxford 91; Society of the Holy Cross, Ty-mawr 88–9; *see also* Benedictines; Dominicans; Franciscans; Taizé Community
community 2, 13, 43–6, 49; *see also* 'being' and 'doing'; communities, religious
Conference, Edinburgh, 1910 *see* Ecumenical Movement
Conference of European Churches 24
conflict, religious 29
Cranmer, Thomas 64
Craven, Margaret 67–8, 105
creation xv, 3, 10; beauty in 4–6
Cruise O'Brien, Conor 103

Dalrymple, William 102
de Chardin, Pierre Teilhard 66–7; *see also* Eucharist; priesthood
deacons 49–51, 69, 71, 73–4, 79–83; distinctive 77; as 'living sacraments' 76–7; as messengers 78; ordained within Methodist Church and some Reformed churches 77; permanent 77; rooted in their community 79; *see also* Church of England; diaconate; *diakonia*
'death of God' theology *see* theology
diaconate xii, xiii, 11, 13, 49–51, 69, 74, 82; in Church of England 78; in Church of Scotland 77; diocesan initiatives on from Chichester and Portsmouth 80; Toyenkirchen project, Norway 82; Wakefield diocese booklet 80
diakonia 49, 50, 82, 86, 92
Diana, Princess of Wales 21; *see also* 'Candle in the wind' (Elton John)
Dominic, St 90
Dominicans (Order of Preachers) xiii, 52, 90
Dulles, Avery 104

Eaton, Gai 100–1; *King of the Castle* 100; Bernard Levin's review 100
Ecumenical Movement 19–20, 77; Edinburgh Conference, 1910 20; Pontifical Council for Promoting Christian Unity 20; Porvoo Declaration 20; *Unitatis Redintegratio* 19–20
Ehrmann Max 5, 102; 'Desiderata' 5
Einstein, Albert 27
Engels, Friedrich 33
episcopacy *see* bishops
Ethiopia 23, 43
Eucharist 12–13, 39, 63–4, 74, 86, 97–9; Teilhard de Chardin on 66–7
Europe 33–4
Eurovision Song Contest 41

Farrer, Austin 39, 65, 76–7, 98–9, 104–6
Ferrar, Nicholas *see* Little Gidding Community

ffrench-Beytagh, Gonville *see* South
   Africa
Fiddes, Paul 104
'first foot' *see* New Year's Eve
First World War 67
Fletcher, Joseph ('new morality')
   19
Fox, Charles James *see* French
   Revolution
Francis, St 20, 30–1, 36, 73, 86, 90
Franciscans xiii, 20–1, 30, 36–7, 85–7,
   89–90, 92; Alnmouth Friary 86, 92,
   95; friars 52; Second Order (St Clare)
   20–1, 36, 87, 91–2; Third Order 20,
   37, 91, 93
French Revolution 31–3, 39; anti-
   clericalism 33; Charles James Fox,
   writing on 31; Vendée 31–2

Geldof, Bob (Live Aid) 23
Gooder, Paula 105
gospel (good news) xiii, xiv, 24, 72
Graham, Brendan 105
Greenbelt 43
Gregory the Great 90
Grumett, David 105

Hague, William 103
Hamlet (Prince of Denmark) 5–6
Hammarskjöld, Dag (United Nations
   Secretary General) 17, 67, 103, 105;
   Markings 17
Hardy, Thomas 4, 7, 102; 'The
   Convergence of the Twain' 4
Herbert, George 73
Hockney, David 18
Hogmanay *see* New Year's Eve
Holliday, John 102
Holly, Buddy 14
Holocaust (Shoah) 3
Holy Land 29
Honecker, Erich 34
Hooke, Robert 85, 106
humanity 13, 34, 37, 39, 43, 47, 49, 53,
   56, 58–9; transformed by death and
   resurrection of Jesus 45; *see also*
   atonement
Hussein, Saddam 3

imagery, rooted in song xiv
'Imagine' (John Lennon song) 28–30;
   see also Lennon, John
Islam xi, 22, 29
Israel 28

James, Eric 104
Jasper, David 102, 103
Jasper, Ronald C. D. 104
Jerome 52, 89
Jerusalem 29
Jesus Christ: atonement through 58–60;
   beatitudes 30–1; incarnation xiv, 11,
   19, 37; life of poverty 20; life of
   service 49; offering of selfhood 40;
   passion 10, 38; as Redeemer 10, 64;
   resurrection 10, 45; role as reconciler
   47–8; sermon on the mount 30
John, Elton *see* 'Candle in the wind'
John XXIII, Pope 17
Judaism 29, 89

Kennedy, John F. 14–15, 17–19
Kennedy, Robert 15, 18
Khrushchev, Nikita *see* Soviet Union
Kilner, Celia 105
Kilvert, Francis 6, 10
King, Martin Luther 15, 18, 23
Kingdom of God 10, 82
Kirk, Kenneth 35, 36, 38, 75, 92, 100,
   103, 106; *Vision of God, The* 35, 92
Klein, Melanie 59

Lampe, Geoffrey 38, 103
Lenin 33
Lennon, John 15, 34, 39, 40, 103;
   'Imagine' song 28–31
Levin, Bernard 54–5, 104, 106; review
   of *King of the Castle* (Gai) 100; review
   of *The Last Temptation of Christ*
   (Scorsese) 54
liberation theology *see* theology
Little Gidding Community (Nicholas
   Ferrar) 73
Liturgical Movement 77
Live Aid *see* Geldof, Bob
Lovland, Rolf 105
Lutheranism 4, 24, 50; Lutherans 82

McLean, Don 14–17, 26–7, 102
Mandela, Nelson *see* South Africa
Mao Zedong 3; biography of 102
Marx, Karl 33, 39; Marxism 36;
    Marxist-Leninism 39
Mayne, Michael 8, 102
Mendel, Gregor 52
Middle East 3, 28
Mirfield, the Resurrection *see*
    communities, religious
mission of the Church 25, 52; *missio Dei*
    (God's mission) 25, 82
Mitchell, Joni 1, 8–11, 102
monasteries, dissolution of the 90
monasticism, religious life 52
Monte Cassino *see* Benedict
Mother Teresa 53
Muir, Edwin 8–10, 106; 'The Child
    Dying' 8–9, 61; 'One Foot in Eden' 9
Murdoch, Iris 35, 103
mystery of God 27

Naudé, Beyers *see* South Africa
Naught for Your Comfort (Trevor
    Huddleston) 25; *see also* South Africa
'new morality' *see* Robinson, John
New Testament 7, 38, 44
New Year's Eve 41–3, 55; 'Auld lang
    syne' 43; *Dinner for One* film 41;
    'first foot' 42; Hogmanay 42
Newton, Sir Isaac 84–5
Nicene Creed 51, 75
Nixon, Richard (Watergate) 18

Old Testament 25
Oppenheimer, Helen 50, 104
ordained ministry xiii, 13, 87
ordination 39, 75, 24
Orthodoxy, Eastern 33
Osborn, J. 105
Oxford, Sisters of the Love of God *see*
    communities, religious

Paine, Tom 31–2
Palestine 69
Parry, Dom David 106
Paton, Alan 25, 103; *Cry, the Beloved
    Country* 25

Paul VI, Pope 19, 21
permanent deacons *see* deacons
Pitt, William 32
Platten, S. G. 104
Pontifical Council for Promoting
    Christian Unity 20
Pope, Alexander 6–8; *Essay on Man*
    6–7
Porvoo Declaration *see* Ecumenical
    Movement
prayer 64, 66–7, 74, 76; contemplative
    prayer 52, 64–5, 67, 97–9
priesthood xii, xiii, xiv, 11–13, 20, 26,
    56–9, 63–4, 66–9, 74, 79–80; priestly
    role of Church in reconciliation 49;
    Teilhard de Chardin's understanding
    of 66–7
priests 76–7; as 'living sacraments' 76–7
projective identification (Melanie Klein)
    59
Python, Monty 54; *Life of Brian* 54

Quoist, Michel 69–70, 105

Ramsey, A. M. (Michael) 36–8, 39,
    63–5, 98, 103, 105; as Archbishop
    of Canterbury 36–7; *The Christian
    Priest Today* xii, 13; introduction to
    Peake's Commentary on the Bible 37;
    Westminster Abbey sermon for
    Franciscan anniversary 36–7
reader ministry xii, 51, 53, 94–5
reconciliation: 57–8, 63; Church's
    vocation in 47–9
redemption 10, 45, 46, 97
Reeves, Ambrose *see* South Africa
Reformation xiii, 20, 49, 90
religious life xii, 51–3, 92–3, 95; *see also*
    communities, religious; Franciscans
    (friars); monasticism; sisters
    (religious)
Religious Society of Friends (Quakers)
    20
representative ministry 50
Riccardi, Andrea *see* communities,
    religious (Sant'Egidio)
Robinson, John 18, 19; *Honest to God*
    18; 'new morality' 19

Roman Catholic Church 19, 20, 32, 46, 77, 90; Bishops' Conferences in Europe (CCEE) 24

Romantic movement *see* Wordsworth, William

Rumour of Angels, A (Peter Berger) 20, 103

sacrament of penance 59; *see also* absolution; priests

Salvation Army 20

science, medical 5

Scorsese, Martin 54; *Last Temptation of Christ, The* 54; review by Bernard Levin 54

Second Order (of St Clare) *see* communities, religious; Franciscans

Second Vatican Council 17, 19–20, 77

Second World War 3, 12, 18, 24, 28, 34, 62, 69, 91

secular humanism 35

secularization 18, 29; Harvey Cox (*The Secular City*) 18; secular humanism 19, 35 September 11, 2001 (New York) 22

sermon on the mount 30

Shakespeare, William 5, 43–4, 54–5, 102, 104

Sharpe, John 104

silence 98; *see also* prayer, contemplative

Simon and Garfunkel 56, 57

sisters (religious) 52; *see also* communities, religious

Smith, Stevie 47–8, 50, 55, 104; 'The Airy Christ' 47

Solidarity *see* Walesa, Lech

solidarity 53, 58; *see also* community

Soskice, Janet Martin 99, 106

South Africa 24–5, 63; apartheid 24–5; Beyers Naudé 24; Bishop Ambrose Reeves 24; Bishop Joost de Blank 24; Council of Churches 24; Desmond Tutu 21, 24, 63; Gonville ffrench-Beytagh 63; Nelson Mandela 24; Trevor Huddleston 24, 25, 52, 63, 91, 103, 104; 'Truth and Reconciliation' process 63

South Bank theology *see* theology

Soviet Union 18–19, 24; Cuban Missile Crisis 18; Nikita Khrushchev 18–19, 33; religion 33–4

Spence, Joseph 105

Spring Harvest 43

Stalin, Josef (Joseph Dzhugashvili) 3, 33

Stewart, Patrick 44

suffering, innocent 2–4, 9–10, 12

syncretism 23

Synod, General 13, 78, 94

Taizé Community 52, 91; Brother Roger 91; Father Max Thurian 91

Taylor, John V.: reflections on Christlike God 38–9, 40, 103

Teresa of Avila, St 52

'The way old friends do' 41–55; *see also* Abba

theiosis 39, 66, 99

theology 64–7, 98; 'Death of God' 19; political 19; liberation 19; South Bank 18

Toyenkirchen *see* diaconate

Toynbee, Philip 88–9, 106

transcendence *see* Jesus Christ, incarnation

Tully, Mark 102–3

Turnbull, H. W. 106

Tutu, Desmond *see* South Africa

Ty-mawr, Society of the Sacred Cross *see* communities, religious

Ulvaeus, Björn 103

Unitatis Redintegratio see Ecumenical Movement

unselfing 35

Vanstone, W. H. 11, 48, 61, 65–6, 79, 102, 104–5; *Love's Endeavour, Love's Expense* 11, 59–60, 61, 102; *The Stature of Waiting* 48, 104

Vickers, Salley 72, 105; *Miss Garnet's Angel* 72

vocation xi, xii, xiii, xiv, 19–21, 23, 26, 49, 51, 54–5, 69, 76, 87, 93–4, 95–6; *see also* religious life

vows, monastic: of hospitality 92; of stability 92

Walesa, Lech (Solidarity trade union) 34, 46

Wantage, St Mary the Virgin *see* communities, religious

Warhol, Andy 18

'way old friends do, The' 41–55; *see also* Abba

Western Europe xii

Westlife 84; 'You raise me up' 84, 87, 96

Whitby, Order of the Holy Paraclete *see* communities, religious

William Pitt the Younger (William Hague) 32, 103

Williams, Charles 39

Williams, Robbie 71–2, 82, 105

Williams, Rowan *see* Canterbury, Archbishops of

Wittgenstein, Ludwig 27, 103

Wooldridge, Mike *see* Ethiopia

Wordsworth, William 7–8, 102

World Council of Churches 20

Yugoslavia, former 24